The Red Suit Diaries

The Red Suit Diaries

A Real-Life Santa
on Hopes, Dreams, and Childlike Faith

Ed Butchart

Fleming H. Revell
A Division of Baker Book House Co
Grand Rapids, Michigan 49516

Published by Fleming H. Revell
a division of Baker Book House Company
P.O. Box 6287, Grand Rapids, MI 49516-6287

Printed in the United States of America

Library of Congress Cataloging-in-Publication Data
Butchart, Ed.
    The red suit diaries : a real-life Santa on hopes, dreams, and childlike faith / Ed Butchart.
        p.   cm.
    ISBN 0-8007-1814-3
    1. Santa Claus. 2. Department stores Santas. I. Title.
GT4985.B87 2003
394.2663—dc21   2003010530

SEP 1 5 2004

16

For Annie

and the God who loves us

The Diaries

Hopes

Dear Sir,

I'm wondering about you -- you can't possibly go to everyone's house in just one night, even though have 24 hours to do it, considering the different time zones. How can you be in so many places at one time? What I mean is, When I was little and went to the mall, I saw you. When I got home, my cousin called me and said that she had just been sitting on Santa's lap at the mall. Get this -- we live an hour and half away from each other! That proves my point! You must have a ton of look-a-likes, or you're not real. But by chance if I'm wrong and you are real, then I don't want anything for Christmas this year. I just want my aunt to be cured of her cancer. And you can't do that only God can make that happen. So I'll pray to him for a miracle. In the mean time could you stop by her house and give her some raspberry truffles? Dark Choclate, please. They're her favorite. I'm sure she'd love to see you. It's been about 40 years. Thanks alot

Your Wondering friend

Mackenzie age 11

Secrets I Must Tell

It was the night before the night before Christmas, the last day of a long Santa season that had begun in October. The clock on the wall showed just a few minutes before 9:00 P.M., and I was struggling to be the Jolly Old Saint Nick every child deserves to meet.

I had something heavy on my heart that night. Mrs. Claus, my beloved wife, Annie, had been in the hospital for three days, and I hadn't been there to sit near her bedside or sleep nights in the cot next to her bed so she wouldn't be alone. I was anxious for this shift to end so I could dash home, change clothes, and head for the hospital. There was a chance Annie would be discharged the next morning, Christmas Eve, and I wanted to be there to take her home. We both could've used a long winter's rest.

11

The patter around Santa's throne had been routine. Kids were lined up, waiting to tell me their wishes, and adults were impatient to have me help make their little ones' dreams come true—at least for the moment. Jolly or not, I was required to be there, so I was working hard not to let the Santa experience seem my obligation or someone else's bore. I even had an "elf" sitting on a stool beside me for good cheer. Trent was a little person, three feet, nine inches tall, seventeen years old, and delightful company. So Trent and I chatted between the interviews with the children, and our exchanges energized me and kept me going, one child after the next.

Then came this one little boy.

He couldn't have been more than five, and he had been watching me intently, hands folded across his chest, for about ten minutes as he moved along with the flow, Mom at his side. Finally it was his turn for the Santa interview. He ambled up the steps and climbed onto my lap, seating himself on my left knee. He stared expectantly into my eyes. This was serious business.

the Red Suit Diaries

"Well, hello," I said, chuckling. The interview had begun.

"Hello," the little guy responded.

"How are you doing?" I asked.

"Fine."

"Well,"—and here came the inevitable question—"have you been a good boy?"

"Umm . . ." The boy paused and looked up at the ceiling. He tapped his chin with his forefinger. "Umm . . ." he repeated, scouring the ceiling.

"What's he doing?" Trent whispered in my right ear.

We followed the boy's eyes to the ceiling to see what was so interesting up there. Nothing. Yet still the little guy was tapping his chin and searching for . . .

Ah, I thought, *he's looking for an answer. Here's a little man giving great thought to a most important question.*

"He's thinking," I whispered to Trent.

"About what?" Trent was incredulous.

"I don't know," I chuckled, "but this ought to be good!"

Suddenly the boy stopped tapping his chin. "Well," he said as his eyes looked intently into mine. "Well," he started over in an effort to get his answer just right, "I had a pretty good August . . ."

Trent fell off his stool, and I burst into laughter as the kid, clearly puzzled, wondered what was so hilarious. Well, it was probably the first honest answer this Santa had ever heard!

Mustering control, I asked, "So what do you want for Christmas?"

The boy grinned big as Christmas and started his list, but I don't remember his reply. My ability to concentrate had left in the face of his startling honesty. He took such an important question seriously and wanted Santa, in whom he had great trust, to get only the truth. Such faith in me! Such hope, despite his eleven bad months!

Regaining composure, I listened intently and admonished, "Well, remember to always be a good boy—and not just in August." Then I sent the little guy on his way back to Dad.

Mom was waiting nearby and couldn't stand it. She just had to find out what her boy had said to cause so much levity. I recounted the exchange in a whisper in her ear.

the ℝed Suit Diaries

"He really said that?" she mused, awed by her baby's candor. She laughed, and Trent and I joined her, the two of us erupting again as Mom bade us farewell.

Just then I realized I had witnessed a miracle of Christmas that my job gives me the privilege to see—an expression of childlike faith and hope, all tied up with a bow, offered in a single whisper or a letter from the heart to a place way up north.

Suddenly gone were my feelings of anxiety and my desire to finish this last night of Santa duties. With heightened expectation I looked to the next child, and the next, for that one magical moment of sheer joy, hope, and belief in all that's good—in promises too good to be true.

These are the moments that convinced me some secrets, like some promises, are too precious to keep to myself. They must be shared. And so begins my open diary to you . . .

In the Beginning . . .

Every Santa remembers his or her very first time in the suit.

I was a senior in high school, working a holiday retail job at Belk's Department Store in my hometown of Greensboro, North Carolina. I had the opportunity to borrow the Belk's Santa costume, and my brother had just the job for me. Come to the house dressed as Jolly Old Saint Nick, he prompted, and help wean Susan—his toddler, my niece—of her beloved blanky. Susan had promised to give up her baby blanket, but only to Santa for one of his elves, and only if Santa himself came to her house to claim the prize.

How could playing Santa and helping my brother hurt anything?

I agreed, imagining my brother and sister-in-law's relief to get rid of that worn-out blanket—and little Susan's delight at getting Santa to herself for a moment. She was sure to be mesmerized. And what fun it would be to play Jolly Old Saint Nick without her ever knowing it was Uncle Ed.

I rehearsed hundreds of greetings throughout what seemed to be a slow day at work. By evening, I was in the spirit of the surprise. I grabbed the suit, really feeling the part, and drove to my brother's neighborhood. I parked in a lot down the street and wiggled into the red slacks and jacket, then adjusted the beard, belt, and hat as I strode up the driveway. My heart was all aflutter as I took a deep breath and rang the bell.

I could hear Susan fumbling with the knob, then I watched her eyes widen as she opened the door. But before I could make my well-rehearsed greeting, she shrieked and raced across the living room, down the hall, and into her room. In a flash she was under the bed.

I looked helplessly at my brother. Bob looked helplessly back. Neither of us had anticipated Susan's alarm about this personal visit from Santa. After all, it was her idea.

For an awkward moment, I stood dumbfounded as Bob sighed and gestured to an overstuffed chair. "Sit," he said perfunctorily. He was just learning to expect the unexpected from toddlers.

So I sat, but not without fears of my own. I'd stuffed the suit with two pillows, my ears were contorted by the strings holding on the long, flowing beard, and my 7 3/8 inch head was forced into a 6 1/4 inch wig. Any minute I feared the buttons on my suit would pop and the wig would squirt off my head, taking all my hair with it.

I held my breath as Bob and my sister-in-law, Virginia, tried talking Susan out from under her bed. They reminded her of her promise and reassured her that Santa loved her and would never hurt her. Then they begged.

Nothing worked.

My spirits were melting, along with the rest of me under all the Santa gear. By the time Bob pulled Susan out from her hiding place to comfort her, I had soaked the pillows and my beard with sweat. *Maybe if Susan sees "Santa" is really Uncle Ed,* I thought, *she might calm down. Of course, that would ruin the Santa surprise for every Christmas after this . . .*

I sweated more over what to do. It only took a minute to see there was no danger of my niece discovering my real identity. There was no way she was coming close enough to find out. With her right arm extended as far as possible, she did offer her precious blanky—from the very tips of her fingers. I reached for the gift, thanking her in the deepest voice I could muster and promising that

18

the ʀed Suit Diaries

one of the elves would be glad to receive such a special blanket.

But Susan, with reflexes set on hyper speed, was already gone.

Laying my finger alongside my nose and giving a nod, I decided it was time for me to go too, if Bob and Virginia were ever to have some Christmas peace.

I left then, not knowing that Susan's screams should have been expected. Seventy-five percent of children from eleven months old to age three scream and cry at the sight of Santa.

But I didn't need a statistic to tell me the most important lesson of this experience. I saw it for myself: The red suit embodies something and someone so big and real that you must confront it or cry. Sometimes things to believe in make you do both. In any case, there is a power in portraying Santa, and with it a responsibility that calls for unconditional love—screams or not.

Embodying something to believe in is not a job for the faint of heart.

The Path to the Throne

Nobody sets out to be Santa Claus. Maybe in Hollywood an actor is selected for the role and goes down to makeup, where an artist sticks on a beard, adds a bit of color to the cheeks and nose, then sends the guy to wardrobe, where a dresser picks out a red suit and—voila!—Jolly Old Saint Nick. Yet like everything else about real life versus Hollywood, becoming Santa just isn't that easy.

Of course, after the encounter with my screaming niece, I had no intention of wearing an all-red suit ever again. In fact, I didn't particularly care for kids, especially little ones and infants. Maybe Susan did me in, or maybe I was just predisposed to be more annoyed than enamored with anyone vulnerable.

In any case, for the next forty years I became more like Scrooge.

I finished college at the University of North Carolina and took my journalism degree into the Marine Corps as a second lieutenant. I donned green or tan suits every day as an infantry unit leader and learned forty-three different ways to kill and survive on the

the Red Suit Diaries

battlefield. Self-sufficiency spoke volumes to me, becoming the quality I admired most. And I learned to love my troops and fellow officers as though my life depended on it—which, of course, it did. This was a limited love, however—a love based only on what someone could do for me.

Then in 1978, I retired from the Marine Corps and began working as a salesman for a medical diagnostics company. Around this time I met a young man attending my church who had cerebral palsy and used a wheelchair. I presumed we would have nothing in common and nothing to talk about, so for about two years I kept our acquaintance to nods in the hallways.

In truth, I was intimidated by the chair.

When we finally had a conversation, I learned this young man was well-read and fascinating company. I began to visit him at his home, an apartment nearby.

On one of those visits, my new friend asked me to change a lightbulb.

Now, I had been decorated in the service by U.S. and foreign generals and had received all kinds of awards for writing and for selling. I thought I was a good man who loved God and treated others Christianly. But none of those rewards or impressions of myself compared with what I suddenly felt while putting in a new lightbulb for someone who couldn't do it himself.

Nothing I had done before in all my self-sufficient military service or church attendance seemed so significant as this. A simple flick of my wrist could be a huge gift. And I was the one receiving—a new sense of value, a "ministry" some might call it, a true purpose.

A light turned on inside of me.

Meeting Mrs. Claus

As if I had been bitten by the Good Deed Bug, I began to change other lightbulbs and do chores around the complex where a number of disabled people lived. Eventually, I found and bought an old Head Start program government van and installed a ramp and tie-downs for wheelchairs so I could give my disabled friends a lift to appointments and social events.

the Red Suit Diaries

Then my daughter, Gail, and I went apartment hunting so I could live in a place where I could bring my friends who were wheelchair users. We looked at twenty-four different places in two weeks without finding one that was even close to being wheelchair accessible.

On one of our fruitless apartment searches, Gail wanted to stop at her bank to make a deposit, and she wanted me to come inside with her to meet the lady who had opened her account. I told her the last thing I wanted to do was meet any lady. I just wasn't interested. I had been hurt enough already when my marriage ended some years ago.

It was too warm to wait outside in the car, though, so I went inside. Gail waved at a beautiful blonde woman whose desk nameplate said "Ann Moore." Immediately I was struck by Ann's beautiful smile— and her face and her sweet, melodic voice. We were introduced as Gail made her deposit, and the conversation turned to our father-daughter mission of the day. Ann asked what kind of place we were looking for; Gail told her we weren't that particular, so long as we could get wheelchairs in the front door.

Startled, Ann looked both of us over again for evidence of wheels.

I explained that I'd been helping out some folks in wheelchairs and that I wanted them to be able to visit us. Ann thought the apartment complex where she lived had some units that opened directly onto the sidewalk. She wrote down the address on her business card and gave it to us.

It turned out the apartment directly below Ann's (though we didn't know it at the time) was wheelchair accessible, so two weeks later we moved in. And within a few weeks of that, Gail was staying with Ann's nine-year-old son, Brian, who was on spring break, while Ann worked.

That week, Gail told me Ann was sick and that I should "do something!" I found Ann flushed, feverish, unable to keep her eyes open, and slurring her words.

"Get ready," I told her and Gail. "We're going to the emergency room."

With a temperature of 104 degrees and an infection out of control, Ann was immediately put on

the Red Suit Diaries

intravenous antibiotics. She would be in the hospital for eighteen days.

It was then and there that Christmas truly began to creep back into my soul.

I began checking in on Ann, and we began talking a great deal. One Sunday we spent the entire afternoon talking. We learned that we each believed in God and that her birthday was July 15, just one day after mine. We shared our pasts, our hopes, and our plans. She told me how she wanted to become a vice president at the bank. I revealed my desire to go to Indonesia as support for a missionary group I'd first become acquainted with during my service in Vietnam.

When I told Ann about my recent experiences with folks living with mobility disabilities, she lit up. She was intrigued to learn that at the place where the folks with disabilities lived, a Bible study group prayed for her at every session.

Once Ann was able to go home, we began to spend even more time together. We went shopping, and she bought an entertainment center after I promised to put it together. As I assembled it, she introduced me to a song by Dallas Holm: "Rise Again."

As we dined out on the fifty-dollar referral award Ann had received because we took the apartment in her complex, I felt like I truly was rising again from what I realized now were ashes. My marriage had ended three years before, after twenty-two years, and for all my bravado about self-sufficiency, I was beginning to realize I longed for someone to share my life with.

Ann's marriage had also ended, seven years before under horrible conditions. One evening we talked about how neither of us wanted to plunge into another relationship. Well, that was what we kept telling ourselves and each other. But in the meantime, Ann, Brian, and I were talking and laughing together. We were becoming a family.

One evening I mentioned calmly, "The only way I would ever consider marrying again would be if I could find someone like you willing to marry me."

Ann looked very thoughtful and responded, "If I found a man like you who would have me, I would get married again too."

the Red Suit Diaries

I startled myself by saying, "Would July 16 be OK?"

She shocked me even more by saying, "Yeah, I think that would be a perfect day."

"Whoa, wait a minute!" I practically yelled. "Did what I think happened, just happen?"

She looked me in the face, smiled brightly, and said, "I think you and I have a wedding to plan. What do you think?"

We each confessed we had liked each other the minute we met, and now we began to tell our friends about our love. Our children, Gail and Brian, were ecstatic. So were Ann's parents.

On July 16, 1983, Annie (my name for her) and I were married at the carillon at Stone Mountain Park, a historic theme park site near Atlanta—after we had celebrated my birthday on Thursday and hers on Friday. And now we were celebrating becoming a couple, partners in marriage, ministry, and life. Our friends and family—and some strangers enjoying the park that day—were all there. Everyone was a gift, and love was celebrated. That's what Christmas is anyway. Love. A gift.

Who says Christmas can't come in July?

The Suffering Santa-in-Making

A few days after our honeymoon, Annie developed an acute pain in her lower abdomen. It got progressively worse, and by midnight we were back in the emergency room. Some strong pain medication allowed her to sleep fitfully on a gurney. I slept below, on the bare terrazzo floor.

The next morning surgeons performed exploratory surgery and found nothing. Mysteriously, following the surgery, the pain was gone.

This was the first of nine times that Annie's abdomen would be opened up, and the first of fifty-two times she would be put to sleep for surgical procedures over the years. She's spent more than one year of days in the hospital, and I've been with her for all but eight of them, sleeping on cots, in chairs, and on the floor.

She too has spent nights by my side in a hospital room—when I had a heart catheterization and an angioplasty, and after a six-bypass open heart surgery.

Neither of our experiences are what folks think of when sugar plums begin to dance in their heads. Yet Annie and I are convinced that suffering has made us better people. How could we understand the dashed hopes, true hurts, and soreness of heart and body that others experience if we'd never experienced them ourselves?

First, the Workshop

Early in our marriage, Annie and I saw my professional life thrive. I had become a very effective salesman, winning several sales awards and big bonuses, but I longed to spend more time with my new disabled friends.

Annie loved spending time with our friends too— she plunged right in and did whatever needed doing. Soon we began to look for more opportunities to help our friends together, and I was determined to devote time to what was becoming my ministry.

Interestingly, the more we did for others, the greater sales I made in my territory, whether I was in it or not. I began to realize that someone up there was looking out for me.

Annie is a great deal responsible for that realization. She proposed we take a step in faith and buy a new, larger van that could accommodate more of our friends in wheelchairs. We decided to use a $250 gift we'd received from a niece of one of our friends to secure the van and trust God to provide what we'd need to make the monthly payments. *Why not?* I decided. *God has surprised me with new friends and a perfect partner for life and work. What might he do when I really step out to do more for him?*

No sooner had Annie and I made this decision than the senior minister, Jack Ballard of Mount Carmel Christian, called us to offer financial help if we could do more for the disabled folks in our congregation.

Annie and I marveled at this request. We hadn't mentioned our plans to Jack or the church. They had called us!

We never did make a personal payment for the van. All the payments were covered—and our faith increased. Soon we really began to dream big. How could we do more?

the $\mathcal{R}$ed Suit Diaries

Annie and I decided the next step would be to minister to disabled folks full-time. On September 26, 1986, we incorporated our efforts with the name Friends of Disabled Adults, Inc. (FODA), determining to repair wheelchairs and other medical equipment, one piece at a time, for folks in need.

Within six months of establishing the incorporation, I quit my sales job and we began to "do FODA," coordinating repairs and seeking equipment donations full-time from our home and church.

Now, some people think it's elves who run Santa's workshop, but for this Santa, my Mrs. Claus is the hub. She nudged me to follow my heart for my friends, and she supported me as I pursued a new dream: earning a degree in theology at Atlanta Christian College.

Using my GI Bill benefits, I had started part-time schooling while I was still working. In the fall of 1987, I began a full course load. It was a daunting task, but I graduated in May of 1989 and was ordained as a minister of the Christian church.

My transformation into Santa, and my embodiment of what so many folks associate with Christmas, was becoming complete. Of course, for me, Christmas is about much more than being Santa—it's what's in your heart, not what's in your workshop.

Next, the Heart and Soul

A year after setting up the workshop, our church asked if I would be Santa at its "Living Christmas Tree" program. The folks at Mount Carmel must've seen me growing into some version of Santa—a character known for giving and loving—because it had been forty years since I'd worn the red suit. I wasn't even sporting a beard (or what Annie and I later would call my "professorial look") at that time.

But nevertheless, I agreed to take on the role, with a few reservations about clamoring kids, and donned what I thought was a beautiful but phony beard.

In the course of the evening, one child in the program's cast gave me a cookie and stood coolly waiting for me to eat it. I forced it through the opening between the mustache and beard and nearly choked to death on the fool thing. I resolved then that I would grow my own beard for the next year's event, and started right away.

Visions of becoming Santa were beginning to take hold of me.

By the next Christmas, 1988, I'd grown a beautiful beard and thought I could do an even more beautiful job portraying Jolly Old Saint Nick.

Then I saw Annie, Mrs. Claus, in action. She loved the children simply and completely, with hugs and pats on the back and an ever-listening ear. *This is what Santa and Mrs. Claus should be,* I thought. *An embodiment of the unconditional love Christ has shown.*

Annie and I talked about it later, how fulfilling it was to see the wonder and joy on the faces of those kids in the program. And how discouraging it was to hear from some folks about less-than-virtuous Santa pretenders around the country who made a living portraying a mean old elf. Then the idea dawned: Wouldn't it be a ministry in and of itself, and an additional source of income (allowing me to concentrate on our growing ministry), to portray a Christlike Santa?

As I toyed with this question, I heard about some Christians who were troubled by the persona of Santa.

I began to research this and discovered that the legend of Saint Nick was rooted in a real person, Bishop Nicholas of Myra, who was known for showering children with gifts as a way of emulating the gifts presented by the magi to Jesus of Nazareth.

Somehow, though, Saint Nicholas became known as Santa Claus over the years, and then was commercialized, as in Clement Moore's poem "The Night Before Christmas" and Hayden Sundbloom's illustrations for a Coca Cola advertisement. Stripped of his Christian origins, Santa was suddenly a strictly pagan figure—and one who interfered with the real meaning of Christmas.

Could I somehow steer attention back to the true story about a bishop in Greece hundreds of years ago—and before that, to the greatest Christmas gift of all time, the baby born of God and a virgin?

And a Child Shall Lead Them

At about this time, I ran into a mother, Barbara Cone, and her Down's syndrome daughter, Annette, at church. The Cones always entered the church through

the Red Suit Diaries

the portico door and went down the steps to the fellowship hall where, one Sunday after services, our friends with disabilities were having lunch with the church staff.

Within moments Annette, a tiny little lady of twenty-eight, handed me a tiny slip of paper.

"Here is my Christmas list, Santa," she announced. "I didn't want to forget to give it to you."

I took the list but was too stunned to reply as she turned and hustled back out the door.

Our senior minister, Jack, walked over to me with a smile. "Wasn't that sweet?" he said as we examined the list together. The top item was a typewriter, but there were other items that would have been on the list of any ten-year-old. Several of us at the table looked over the list and made similar comments before I tucked it into my shirt pocket and went about my afternoon.

At church services that evening, Jack set a file folder on the pulpit and looked right at me. "I had a message all prepared for tonight," he said, thrusting the folder on a shelf under the podium, "but I'm going to talk about something else. At lunch today I was privileged to witness a beautiful moment . . ."

Jack went on to tell about Annette and her list. He described the look on her face as the ultimate look of faith and trust, and then he related Jesus' words about how little children and their faith are examples of the kingdom of heaven. He talked about how we adults could learn valuable lessons about faith and trust by watching kids as they interact with Santa Claus. And he spoke about how Santa could be an example of the unconditional love of Christ.

Then he asked if I still had Annette's list with me.

Stunned, I fished in my pocket. As I stepped forward with the list, Jack asked those in attendance to meet with me when the service was over so each person or family could pick one item off the list and bring it to me the following Sunday. He suggested that I could arrange for Santa to make a house call on Annette before Christmas.

The moment the service ended, I was nearly smothered by people wanting to be a part of this special Christmas. One member, whose family owns a funeral home, said he could contribute an IBM Selectric typewriter. Other people agreed to get the rest of the items. Suddenly, the list was covered.

the Red Suit Diaries

I don't think I have ever felt such love emanating from a crowd as I did that night.

The next Sunday everyone brought their gifts to me, and I loaded up the van. And it was quite a load, since some of the items had been duplicated by overeager folks. Annie and I decided that we would take everything to Annette, even if there were two or more of some items.

On December 23, Annie and I found our way to Jim and Barbara Cone's house in rural Henry County. I was quite overcome with anticipation as I loaded Annie down with gifts and got all I could carry. I rang the doorbell and wondered how Annette would react.

She opened the door, then quite matter-of-factly said, "Mama, it's Santa Claus. I told you it would be him."

There was that look of complete faith and trust again. She stepped aside to let us come in, then motioned us into the living room. We sat down, depositing our burdens all around us on the floor. Jim and Barbara joined us, and we immediately went right to work, giving Annette the bounty. She beamed. It wasn't as if she thought *maybe* we would bring those items. She absolutely *knew*—she knew it would all be there and that Santa would bring it all to her.

Annie and I were thunderstruck by Annette's faith and trust. What if believers could have that same trust and confidence in the promises of Christ? What if everyone just *knew* that what he said was true and that he could be trusted?

I began to believe that sharing God's love with kids could be a calling for a man who looked like Santa Claus and who had a lot of love to share, like Bishop Nicholas so long ago. Annie and I discussed how we could use that look and that love as a ministry. We discussed it for several days and weeks after Christmas, and we agreed that next year I would really work on that role for the Living Christmas Tree program.

We had no way of knowing that the role would become much more than we had ever dreamed.

Discovered

In September of 1989 Annie and I were eating at a Chinese restaurant in Stone Mountain, and I noticed that a woman three tables away couldn't take her eyes off me. I began to feel uncomfortable. No one had ever checked me out so blatantly. Had we met before, and I just didn't remember? I told Annie, who didn't recognize her either.

After the woman and her friend got up to leave, she stopped at our table. "Are you a professional Santa?" she asked.

I told her no, I was not a professional, but that I would be interested in what she had to say.

It turned out she was a recruiter for a company that placed Santas in malls all over the country. She called me later and made me an offer to go to a mall in Fort Lauderdale for five weeks, all expenses paid. I told her no. I couldn't be away from my ministry that long.

Then I called a friend at an advertising agency, and he put me in touch with a talent agent. The agent sent me to Gwinnett Place Mall, north of Atlanta.

Illusions at the Mall

When Ted at the talent agency scheduled me to go to Gwinnett Place Mall to meet the public relations folks and the boss of the Christmas crew, who managed the multiple Santas, I thought, *What in the world?*

It turned out that there were three Santas working four-hour shifts to fill up a twelve-hour day. Oh ho, I fretted. How would my portrayal of Old Saint Nick measure up? I agonized over what to wear and what to do about my hair.

Who knew Santa could be so concerned about appearances?

My main concern, though, was more about authenticity than appearances. While I knew I wasn't nearly authentic enough, I didn't know what to do about it.

"Just go," my sweet Annie said, "and be yourself."

"But if I'm just myself, and they find out how I feel about kids, they'll never hire me."

Finally I settled on a red knit shirt and took off for the mall. Unfamiliar with the place, though, I wound up walking through most of the stores, searching for the corporate offices. Along the way adults and kids alike did double takes.

I was surprised.

Not as surprised as the staff was when Santa showed up early at their desks, followed soon after by another

Santa. I introduced myself to Santa No. 2, whose name was Don—a fellow about my size and age, and bald like me, though not wearing glasses like mine. *Well*, I thought, *this takes care of my concern about how all of us Santas could make a transition without folks noticing.*

Then the Santa No. 3 arrived.

Ernest was about half the size of Don and me. He was at least in his midseventies, with an obvious hearing impairment and a beard that, at best, could be described as scraggly. He hid the top of his head under a cowboy hat and was wearing cowboy boots. Immediately, he asked if Don and I were rookies, then he launched into telling us that he was the most experienced and popular Santa in Atlanta. He lectured us on how to "do Santa," and as rookies we listened attentively, because we knew we had a lot to learn.

Then our supervisor arrived, a pleasant young woman who had been working at the mall for several seasons. It was clear she had a better idea of what we were supposed to do than Ernest did. She gave us a booklet, which outlined our performance requirements, and told us to read it carefully later. Then she asked what shifts we wanted to work, and we divvied up the days. Ernest would take the first shift from 10:00 A.M. to 2:00 P.M. I would then work from 2:00 to 6:00 P.M. And Don, who had a full-time day job, would take over from 6:00 to 10:00 P.M. We had a short group interview with the mall director of public relations, and then our boss showed us where we would park, enter the mall, and don our Santa costumes.

We were all walking through the mall together when it hit me that here were three guys all looking like Santa pretenders. Now we were *really* getting the stares. I felt uncomfortable with the thought that kids were watching and wondering just what was going on.

Our boss showed us the dressing area that was in an empty store and gave us a chance to try on the very nice costumes the company required us to wear. Then she took us to where we would park and make our way to the dressing area.

I was disappointed to learn that we would have to walk across the mall right in front of the Sears main entrance to get from parking to dressing. The plan was that we would each make our way to the dressing

the ℛed Suit Diaries

area, change into costume, and wait for the Santa we were replacing to leave the throne and walk down to the dressing area.

Five minutes later the "new" Santa would leave the dressing room and head for the throne. (I was still worried about how it would look for me to walk out that door after elf-sized Ernest had walked in.) And, of course, then the "old" Santa had to change clothes, walk across the mall, and leave. But he would still have on his beard!

After the tour Ernest suggested that we eat a snack at a mall restaurant, so back up the mall we went. We got so much attention that I resolved then and there never to be seen anywhere in public with another Santa pretender. (I have walked out of many stores and restaurants since then.)

I brooded over these things all the way home.

"You know," Annie gently told me later, "those things would only concern a man who really, really cared about kids."

"Hmmm," I responded. "Are you suggesting that I may be about to blow my tough image?"

"No," she answered, "I am suggesting that maybe your image is different than what you perceive it to be."

The Big "Do"

Just before our boss left the three of us, she took me aside and suggested I call a woman named Joyce at a hair salon called the Hair Force in Perimeter Mall. I didn't need her to tell me that my hair wasn't quite right. The next day I made the call.

Joyce told me she had one appointment left at 10:00 A.M. on the day before my first Santa shift. She also told me she would be fixing the hairdos of two other Santas the same day.

When the day of my appointment arrived, I played it smart and found the right mall entrance so I was just steps from the salon. My feeling of safety was short-lived, though, when I saw that the door and most of the outside walls of the Hair Force were glass—everyone could see the other two Santas in all their glory, in separate stages of getting their dos done.

Joyce was frantically busy but cordial as she directed me to a chair and said, "Sit."

I sat and began to check out this foreign environment. I spoke to the other two Santas, and we shook hands. One asked me if I was a rookie, and I nodded agreement. He launched into a profanity-laced description of what it was like to have hundreds of children crawling across your lap. I learned from what he said, but it had nothing to do with his words. His behavior toward me, the staff of the shop, and the female customers was so offensive, I learned an awful lot about what kind of Santa not to be. No woman or child should ever hear such talk from Santa.

Fortunately, the other Santa was a much better role model. He was starting his second season at a mall in Cincinnati; when we were able to get away from the roar of old foul mouth, he gave me some significant pointers.

"Don't try to pick up every kid off the floor, and don't expect every kid to be happy about getting on your lap," he instructed. "Make sure you know where every kid's hands are all the time so they can't grab your beard when you're not looking."

Now, all this time, Joyce was running from one of us to the other, frantically washing, rinsing, bleaching, rewashing, toning, drying, rebleaching, rewashing, retoning, redrying, curling, brushing, picking, and spraying.

At fifty-something, I had never gone through such torture before, but I could see the results of the other guys ahead of me, so I sat still. My fellow Santas didn't look much alike, but they did appear like Old Saint Nick. This was another lesson: Not all Santas look alike, but they can still fit the part.

Finally, Joyce said, "What do you think?" She spun my chair around to face the mirror. I was shocked! Amazed! Staring back at me was a beautiful Santa!

It was a remarkable transformation, and I thought I had finally found my calling. Here was somebody I really wanted to be, not just look like. I felt myself filling up with love, and I could hardly wait to show it to every kid I met.

As I put on my coat, Joyce handed me some Nexxus shampoo and conditioner and a statement of services. I was shocked: $104.65! *Becoming Santa isn't without its*

the Red Suit Diaries

price, I thought as I began trying to recall every step in the process so I could ask my Annie to make me as beautiful as she made me happy.

I left the mall thirty minutes after the other Santas. And now there were more than stares. There were smiles, waves, and looks of adoration—not just from the children, but from adults as well, even those who had no kids with them.

Later, as I walked into the Sunday school party already in progress at the church, there were more stares—a moment of "who is that?" Then, recognition. Still, I looked so different that people I had known for years reacted to the "new" me. There was stand-offishness, as if I were a celebrity, and I realized I was going to have to get used to people treating me like I really was somebody.

Thank goodness Annie had a different reaction. She knew it was still me—the me she saw before the new do, the me she loved unconditionally and knew could in turn love her unconditionally from a Santaland throne or a workshop repairing wheelchairs. What makes a Santa, after all, is not the do, but the heart.

First Day

It was a restless night as I tried to protect my brand-new $104.65 hairstyle. I didn't want the appearance at the Sunday school party to be the only use I would get out of my new do investment.

The day dawned clear and cool, and I went about my morning routine, working on a few wheelchairs in the workshop before fretting over the transition at the mall—from a small, skinny Santa, to me, a somewhat "healthier" version.

I had to be "on the throne," as all Santas call their post, at 2:00 P.M., and I did my best to protect my do, choosing a button-front shirt so as not to muss my hair. I kissed my Annie good-bye, put on a red jacket, and got into the van. Santa doesn't always use reindeer.

I made it to the second traffic light, almost a mile from the house, when a green Volvo waiting to make a left turn from the other direction ran a red light. The driver turned right in front of me, and I only had time to think, *Boy, I'm glad I have my seat belt on!* as we crashed. The right front corner of the Volvo hit my front bumper just right of center. It was a significant jolt. I saw the other driver ricocheting around in his front seat because he didn't have on his seat belt, so I jumped out of the van.

Suddenly I realized something else. Here was Santa, involved in an accident in the middle of the intersection of Memorial Drive and Rays Road, a very busy intersection! I checked to make sure the other driver was OK; he wasn't hurt but was significantly embarrassed. Then I realized the van was not driveable and that I was going to be late arriving for my throne shift.

I went to the Krispy Kreme on the corner and, brushing off the stares and comments, used the phone to call Annie and tell her to bring me another vehicle. I then called the mall office and asked them to get the word to the Santa crew that I'd had an accident and would be there as soon as I could.

Annie and Brian arrived with another van almost before the police arrived. So here I was, standing in the middle of the intersection with the other driver and the policeman exchanging insurance information while cars swirled around us. I looked into some of them and saw smiles, stares, and fingers point-ing. Some rolled down their windows and shouted comments like, "What happened, Santa, break your sleigh?"

"Really funny, wise guy!" I wanted to say, but didn't.

I told the policeman my predicament, so he told me to go on, that he would give the other driver a ticket for failure to yield right of way and would give all the information to Annie. I was never so glad to get into a vehicle in my life!

Driving like a cautious maniac, I got to the mall just a few minutes after my due time on the throne. I parked in the designated spot, entered through a service door, and went down the service hall to the door into the mall. I opened it just a crack so I could assess the people traffic and the best way across to the dressing room, then made a mad dash for the other door. One of the elves was waiting there for me.

She asked if I was OK, then said she would tell the head elf that I was there and that the exchange could be made.

I frantically jumped into my costume pants and coat, pulled on my new boots, wrapped my new leather belt and buckle I had made myself around my middle, grabbed a hat, changed to my new character glasses, and started to stroll around the empty store, trying to calm down.

In a moment Ernest came in the door, accompanied by two other elves. He asked if I was OK and offered to take my shift for me if I was hurt. I assured him I wasn't hurting anywhere. He then gave me a crowd report, which didn't even register. (I would soon learn to pay close attention to that information.) I stepped through the door into the mall, and my Santa career was under way.

My heart was beating like mad from all the exertion, and I was sweating profusely. I tried to walk calmly along with the elves, when all I really wanted to do was run! But I waved casually at folks along the way and stopped to pat the head of a couple of kids.

And then we were there.

I walked over and sat down on the throne, which I was seeing for the first time. It was a white, throne-shaped seat, and for the moment I felt quite well seated. (I would come to value very much the design and padding characteristics of throne chairs.) The head elf said, "Are you ready, Santa?" I nodded yes, and she lifted the first child of my career onto my lap.

He was a boy of about five, well dressed and smiling pleasantly. I smiled back and suddenly went blank. I couldn't think of anything to say to him. I sat smiling, and he sat waiting for me to ask him something, anything! I sat transfixed for at least a full minute. Then the chief elf came up and tapped me on the shoulder.

Leaning near my ear she said, "Are you OK?"

"Yeah," I said.

"Well, talk to the kid, smile at the camera, do something!"

I turned to the camera, smiled as best I could after such a comment, and the flash went off. That jolted me back to my senses, and I said to the kid, "How are you?"

"Fine," he answered. Then he had a question. "You want to know what I want for Christmas?"

the ℛed Suit Diaries

I almost hugged and kissed him! That was what I couldn't think to say! He had come to my rescue and didn't even realize it.

"Yes, of course," I answered. "I want very much to hear what you want for Christmas."

The boy launched into an elaborate, well-thought-out and carefully memorized list. I heard almost none of it because I was trying to gather my wits for the rest of the day. When he finished I managed to say that he should be a good boy and I would see him later. Then, before I could take a breath, here was another kid on my lap.

So went the routine. Kid arrives on lap. Smile at camera. Flash. Ask, "What do you want for Christmas?" Listen (or at least appear to). Tell them to be good and reach for the next kid. I was doing OK.

But the boys kept mumbling an unintelligible series of sounds that I couldn't for the life of me figure out. Then at the end of my shift, an older than usual boy who didn't have marbles in his mouth said those sounds, and I almost caught it.

I asked him to repeat it, and he said, very slowly, like he was talking to some complete dolt who was also hard of hearing, "Teenage . . . Mutant . . . Ninja . . . Turtles!" I repeated it back to him, and he said, "Yeah, that, and lots of them!" I had no earthly idea what he was talking about, but I agreed that they would be on his list. I also knew that the moment I got home, I was plunging into the JCPenney Wish Book for some intense study!

The girls had their own set of mystery words. I could make out "Barbie" and heard that almost every time. Then I began to make out "Baby Alive," "Baby Tumbles," "Baby All Gone," "My Pretty Kitty," and others, but I still knew that the evening would be spent hitting the reference books.

Then, suddenly, mercifully, my shift was over. I hadn't even had time to check my new Mickey Mouse watch when the chief elf stopped the line and said, "Time for a break, Santa." I eased into a standing position on shaky legs. There had been approximately two hundred kids on my lap, and I could feel it in my bones and muscles.

The chief elf said, "You did fine, Santa, for your first time. You'll get the routine down in a day or two and be a good Santa."

the Red Suit Diaries

I uneasily walked off the set and headed for the dressing room. I didn't know whether to feel encouraged or embarrassed.

Don was dressed and waiting when I got there. I gave him a crowd report and asked him if he knew what Teenage Mutant Ninja Turtles were. He said he figured it was some kind of toy. I told him I was going to do some research, and he agreed that was a good idea.

When I got home, Annie was dying to hear about my adventures that day, and together we plunged into the Wish Book. I learned all about Teenage Mutant Ninja Turtles, Batman gear, computer games, and dolls. Thus began a new lifestyle of studying all the toy fads and trends.

When we finished the study session and closed the Wish Book, I turned to Annie and thoughtfully asked, "Don't any of the kids ask for bicycles, baseball gloves, roller skates, and fruits and nuts and candy anymore?"

She didn't know.

Years later, the answer is still, "No!"

Hopes

Champion Screamer

The foul mouth at the beauty shop had warned me that 90 percent of the kids from a year to three years of age would be screamers. I found out that he was very close to right. My personal statistics would say that about 75 percent of kids from eleven months to three years are afraid of Santa. Their reactions range from quiet fear to outright terror. Their verbal expressions of that fear have similar ranges.

Some settle for being "Mama climbers." I have seen kids take one look at me, grab their mom (or dad if he's closer) around the knee, and climb right up her body all the way to her shoulders. A few even make it to sitting on her shoulders. I expect someday to see one of them literally sitting on top of his mother's head, maybe even standing on it.

Some just scream, piercing sounds that blow the wax out of my ears. Some simply cry. Others get on my lap quietly and answer part of my questions, then start to cry. And then there are some children who are forced into my lap by a mom or dad who has been waiting for over an hour and wants a picture of Santa, no matter what. Those are the really dangerous situations.

When these kids begin to kick their feet, my shins take a vicious beating. I've been slapped, punched, kicked, head-butted, and generally abused. But so far, in all these years, there has been only one World Class, All-Time, Gold Medal Champion Screamer.

Her mom and dad attended Mount Carmel Christian Church and were friends of ours. We would see their child Jill only occasionally, since she was always in the children's activities. We remembered when she was born and had watched her grow up to be a rambunctious three-year-old. She had always treated me with caution, and I had never gotten close to her at all.

Her mom asked me where I was Santa, and I told her Gwinnett Place Mall and gave her my schedule. A few days later I looked down the line, and there they were—Mom, Dad, Jill, and her big brother, who was six years old. Jill was watching me very warily, with her arms akimbo.

A few more kids went by quickly, and then it was their turn. Brother came easily and was lifted onto

my left leg. Mom picked up Jill and started for me
. . . and the fun began!

Jill let out a piercing scream that could've been heard in the parking lot. She started to flail her arms and kick her feet. She was about to destroy the beautiful dress she had on when I pushed her away to protect myself and her brother from bodily harm.

Mom had clearly decided that she had invested forty-five minutes in that line and wasn't giving up. She took Jill aside and had a little talk with her. She (Jill, not Mom) calmed down some, and here they came again. Same result, only more of everything. Big brother still sat quietly on my lap, watching the whole show with a detached expression. Jill ran to Dad and Mom and stood with her hands on her hips. I called Mom over and suggested that they all sit down on the bench close by and watch for a while. Maybe if Jill saw that I wasn't hurting any other kids, then she would calm down. They took me up on that offer, and all moved to the bench.

That didn't prove to be a real good idea, because some of the other kids in line had seen or heard the

the $\mathcal{R}$ed Suit Diaries

scene and decided that maybe Jill was on to something. They screamed too!

I knew *that* was not going to reassure Jill, and soon
her mother, realizing she would have to wait until
Jill was at least seven years old, came up to me and
asked if she could sit on my lap and hold Jill on her
lap. That was a common solution to such a problem,
so I readily agreed, suggesting that she pick Jill up,
face the camera, and back up toward me. I would
then reach out and guide her to a safe landing.

She picked up Jill over by the bench about ten yards
away and began a slow walk backward toward me.
She was pointing out decorations and trying to keep
Jill distracted as she ambled along. Her husband was
giving her arm and hand signals to keep her in my
general direction. *Aha,* I thought, *we might just pull this
off!* She got close enough for me to reach out and grab
her belt, and I gently directed her to a landing. She
sat down very slowly and pointed to the camera.

I was trying to hide behind Mom and was going to
look out from behind the off shoulder as soon as the
camera person was ready. It was all going so smoothly,
but just as I was about to look around toward the

camera, Jill turned her head around, looked over her mom's shoulder, and there I was!

Complete pandemonium, instantly! Screaming, fighting, kicking—everything I had seen before on different kids was included in this one. She was like that famous rodeo horse that has never been ridden. She got me twice with her heels, and beat her mom to a pulp.

And then in the middle of it, here came Dad and brother. They jumped into camera range, smiled, and off went a flash.

I began to wonder what that picture would look like, but I never found out. Jill was screaming so loud that everyone in the mall was gathering to see what on earth was happening. Several families in the line left, knowing their little one would never sit on the lap of that Santa. "What did he do to her, anyhow?"

Usually, when a screamer gets out of sight of Santa, he or she stops screaming. Not Jill. Her folks walked her away down the ramp, and she kept screaming. I could hear her for what seemed like ten minutes as her family made its way toward an exit. Finally, mercifully for me and everyone in the mall, the exit door closed. At least then, the noise was outside.

Unfortunately there was a ripple effect. Every one of the kids under three began to scream bloody murder like Jill.

I always hoped Jill's screaming would stop, but it's an occupational hazard that follows me even outside of the Santa setting. You see, Jill's family attended our church for several years, and after this incident I hoped she would one day get over her fear of me. But despite her parents' best efforts, it never happened.

Anytime Jill would come into the auditorium, which seated almost three thousand, she would stop at the door and scan the room. If she saw me anywhere, she would be gone like a flash out the door. She could be persuaded to come into the auditorium with the children's choir to sing, as long as I was seated at least halfway back. But she would always keep her eye on me. If I made any move that even seemed to be toward her, she was out the door!

Maybe someday when she is twenty or so, I might find out just why she was so afraid. Until then, I will have my memories, a few bruises, but very clean ears.

Dreams

Dear santa claus,

I hope you are doing good IN the North pole.
How maNy elves do You have? How maNy
Toys do They make IN a day?
when you deliver preseNts oN christmas
eve, how many Times do you refillyour
slay? If someone doesn't have a chimney, how do you get
IN? Have you ever set off somtone's alarm systim?
Just woNdering.

I believe iN you even though Johnny Whitcomb
doesNt. Do you believe iN God? I do, and
I Think you are his helper.
I will see you sooN. My house is the yellow ohe
with white shutters. I'll leave you out some
choclit milk this year. I hope You like it.
I like red rider bb guns, iN case You were
woNdering.

LoVe, mitchell, age 8

The Gangster

I knew I was in trouble the minute I saw him. He had a suspicious scowl on his face and his arms were folded tightly across his chest. He was at least six years old, the skeptical age, and was talking out of the side of his mouth to a companion who waited behind him in the line.

I tried to prolong the interview with the kid on my lap while I sized up this little gangster and tried to decide what to do. The photographer gave me the signal to hurry up, and I ended the interview and motioned for the toughie to come to my lap. He didn't look me in the face at first and kept his arms tightly folded as I set him on my left leg.

I asked him what his name was, and he answered me in a near growl that caught me so off guard that I didn't catch what he had said. Then I asked him if he had been a good boy. He turned and looked back at his companion, and I saw a look of expectation on the other lad's face. Then, suddenly, his arms were unfolded, and with a scream straight out of Rambo, he whirled and grabbed my beard with both hands and gave a snatch downward, nearly tearing my head off.

I let out a yell myself and grabbed him by the hair on the back of his head and gave a quick pull of my own.

"Owww!" he hollered. "That hurts!"

"Of course, it hurts," I said. "It always hurts when you pull real hair."

With that, the gangster looked intently at my beard, examining each hair he could sort out. Then he turned to his friend and blurted, "It's real, it's really real! This is him! This is the real Santa!"

The boy launched into one of the longest memorized lists I've ever heard. Not only did he have it memorized, it was arranged in order of priority, a fact he made sure I understood. Clearly, he was a man on a mission.

After his friend had laid his list on me, I realized there was a mother along with them. She emerged from the line after the kids had taken their candy canes, and ushered them away, apologizing for her son. Just the previous weekend her boy had snatched the phony beard off another Santa, she explained, so she had looked at several malls for a Santa who looked "really real."

My face still stung, but I reassured this mom that beard-pulling had been tried before and would surely be tried again (though I hoped with less force). In a way, I said, the incident was a compliment.

Santa Meets Big John

One of my favorite Santa gigs revolves around the two children's hospitals in Atlanta. They each have a Christmas celebration to raise funds: a festival of trees at Egleston Hospital for Children, and an event called Art of the Season at Scottish Rite Children's Hospital.

Now, Art of the Season, held in downtown Atlanta, starts the day after Thanksgiving and runs for ten consecutive days. It's a creative idea that gives kids a chance to be creative making Christmas decorations and gifts for their parents and friends. It's become so popular that elementary school classes, scout units, and families now attend en horde.

Each shift of volunteers at Art of the Season works half a day, so I have to train a new crew twice a day. But it's fun to meet folks from all over Atlanta, in all kinds of businesses, and to watch them enjoy the encounters with the kids.

It's also interesting to observe how kids behave away from their parents. There are even differences in the way some schools' kids behave compared to other schools' kids of comparable age, sex, and racial composition. It's obvious that different schools have different rules of discipline, and that those rules continue to apply (at least in some cases) away from school.

Another interesting finding is that kids behave differently alone than they do in a group. Many times a class will come to see Santa, and I will interview them individually first. At that time they are completely in control, courteous, polite, and considerate.

Then after the last kid in the class has finished, the teacher or a parent will flourish a camera and say,

"Group shot!" Immediately, that group of individuals morphs into a mob. They charge toward the stage, fight their way over each other to sit on my lap, and nearly turn my chair over in the process.

Once they get settled, they often snatch my hat off and put it on their heads. Some kids have even grabbed my glasses off, run their hands down my back and inside my coat. And my beard is always fair game for a pull or two.

On more than one occasion, I have gotten out of my chair and walked off the stage. I tell an adult or two to get them under control if they want a picture. On a couple of occasions I have left the set and walked over to the snack bar just to show I am not going to put up with any kid's misbehavior.

Fortunately, those occasions are rare; most of the time we have a lot of fun together.

Not all the kids are elementary-school-sized either. Every year there has been a group of about twenty adults who come from a center for mentally impaired folks.

The first year they came to see Santa in groups of two or three at a time, and each person in turn had his or her picture taken. And each one of them said with a lilting laugh, "Big John is coming to see you!" It sounded like a warning, maybe, or a promise, or I don't know what.

But it had a clear statement of expectation, of anticipation, of wonder.

After I had heard this same thing about fifteen times, I began to be more than a little curious about this Big John character. *Just how big could he be?* Still, I wasn't particularly concerned. My lap had been load-tested by two of my larger friends to a limit of seven hundred pounds; I had learned that if I have my lower leg vertical and my upper leg parallel to the floor, I can handle a lot of weight. If a large person sat down when I wasn't ready, though, I could very easily pull a muscle in my leg or maybe even break it.

At around 4:00 I looked up, and there was Big John in the line. He was not the biggest person I had ever seen, but he was surely the biggest I'd ever seen in a line waiting to sit on my lap! One of the staff people with the group came up to me and made the introduction. "This is Big John."

"Yeah," I said, "I figured that out by myself."

"He really wants to sit on Santa's lap, but he weighs 427 pounds. We'll understand if you don't want to do it."

I looked at him, and he had a wonderful, sweet smile on his face and a look of anticipation, like he was about five years old and had a real message for me.

"Yeah," I told the staff lady, looking her in the eye. "I'm sure you would understand, but I'm not sure he would. I can't disappoint that boy. I'll handle him, no problem."

Big John came up the steps, and all the other people from the place were arrayed around the set, cheering him on. He came to me and turned around. I made sure my leg was situated and guided him to sit down. I immediately made an important discovery. My two friends had obviously not put their full weight on either of the legs they sat on. But Big John made no effort to reduce my load; he sat down with his full weight on my left leg.

I wasn't sure what was going to give way first—my knee joint, hip joint, or thigh bone—but I was sure something was going to disconnect from something.

I tried to position Big John so that his weight was more toward my knee and could be concentrated on my lower leg structure, but he wound up dead center on my thigh bone. The strain was immediate.

Fortunately, I have a very high pain threshold, so I was able to smile for all the pictures everyone was taking. I asked Big John what he wanted for Christmas, and he smiled but didn't say anything. As soon as the pictures were done he stood up, reached around his considerable self, shook my hand, and made his way off the stage. The crowd cheered.

So did I.

Big John has come back every year since. And I have handled him every time. The happy look on his face as he walks away makes any associated physical pain seem like nothing. Well, OK, almost nothing. Dreams can do that.

Precious Moments

Someone once said about flying that it was "hours and hours of boredom interspersed with moments of sheer terror." Being a Santa is kind of like that;

except it is more like hours and hours of boredom interspersed with moments of sheer joy. Moments that are so precious they shouldn't be known only to "The Man." They should be shared. That's why I'm writing this book. I'd like everyone to share in all those precious moments.

After you've been at it for a while, all the kids begin to look alike and sound alike, and most ask for the same things. Don't get me wrong. They are all beautiful kids, and most are well-behaved. But the vast majority of them are very much alike.

Then comes that precious moment. Some of them you have already read about, and there will be more. Right now I am going to tell you about a precious moment that even looked like a Precious Moment . . . doll, that is!

I saw her when she was about third from next in the line. She was very tiny, about the size of a two-year-old, and she had a round face and rounded eyes that made her look exactly like a Precious Moments doll. She had her arms folded across her chest and was studying me with the gaze an archaeologist must use when she makes a new discovery. In spite of her size, there was a maturity about her that made me discard my normal apprehension about whether she would actually sit on my lap. Somehow, I just knew that she wouldn't be frightened.

When it was her turn she walked right up to between my knees with a shy smile on her face. She stopped, pirouetted around, facing away from me, and lifted her arms for me to pick her up. I could not believe how light she was as I set her on my left knee. I said with a chuckle, "Well, he llo."

"Hello," she responded in a lilting, musical voice.

"How are you doing?" I asked.

"I am doing very well, thank you," she answered. "I have been a very good little girl too." She smiled. She had the biggest, bluest eyes I had ever seen.

The whole time she was on my lap, her fingers were doing spider push-ups against each other. I didn't want this precious moment to end. I looked up for a parent and spotted a dad, beaming with pride.

I called him over and said, "Tell me about this little lady, Dad." He told me her name and said she was three years old. I told him that it was just such moments that made sitting on the throne for hours worth it all.

I asked her what she wanted for Christmas, and she gave me a standard list of Barbies, a doll, and some other items. And then she said, "I want you to bring something very special for my mommy and daddy, because they are so good to me."

I said, "Have they been very good?"

She nodded vigorously and said, "Yes, very, very good."

When the visit was over, I told Dad to bring her back to see me sometime.

About a week later they came again, and we had a great visit. She had forgotten some items she wanted, so we added them to her list. Then I lifted her down to the floor.

Dad stepped up to me and said I was a wonderful Santa and that he would like to talk to me. I gave him a ministry business card, and they left.

I got very excited, wondering what kind of fabulous offer he was going to make. I could see myself headed to fame and fortune in Hollywood, in a movie or in commercials. I could hardly wait to hear from him.

A few days later, with me about to give up on him, he did call. He made an appointment to come see me, and when the time came, I was very excited.

Alas, when we finally got past the "you're a great Santa" comments and got down to his business offer, it only took me a few seconds to recognize the pitch.

Unfortunately for him I'd already heard all about Amway.

My Kind of North Pole

During my second season at Gwinnett Place Mall, I decided I didn't want to work a mall again. I didn't like the emphasis on getting people to buy photographs. We seemed to have become a picture factory, and I wanted to spend more time with the kids.

I had already resolved to find another venue when I got a call from Linda Jackson, the personnel director at the Atlanta area's Stone Mountain Park, a historic theme park. Linda had heard about me and wanted me to be Santa at the employee children's party.

To someone else it may have been just a job at a party, but for me it was an audition, a chance to show the powers-that-be what a Santa ought to be. Annie and I had been married at the carillon in the park, and we had a Stone Mountain address. I really wanted to be the park Santa!

On the day of the party I arrived early, well rested and pumped up to be my most charming. Then the park crew showed me where I would sit. I blanched— a low Queen Anne chair that was going to be agony! I couldn't get my legs in the best position for supporting all those kids.

Oh well, I told myself, *you can take it. This will only be for two hours.*

The kids began to arrive, and I began to throw on the charm. I was loving, animated, kind, cheerful. I had been a good Boy Scout, after all!

Just when I thought I was being my most impressive, I saw Linda talking to a man who looked like he was a boss of some kind. At that moment, into the room came a man and his son whom I knew from church. *Here's a chance to shine,* I thought. They'd be happy to see me. Surely they would know who I was. The boy, about six years old, watched several kids as they talked to me, and then he got into line, his dad by his side. When it was their turn, the boy got onto my lap, and Dad stood nearby. It was a routine interview, and neither of them showed any glimmer of recognition. When the interview was finished, they moved into the room where the refreshments were located.

I couldn't believe they didn't even recognize me (and the next Sunday Dad confirmed this). I thought my efforts to impress my employers were dashed. *Oh, well,* I decided, *it's best just to make the children happy.*

When the two hours were almost over, I noticed Linda talking to two other women over by the door. Somehow I sensed something was happening. After a few more interviews it was time to go, and I started for the door.

The two women stopped me as I was heading out— Kay Thweatt, the public relations director, and Sue Stoll, director of special events. After several questions, they asked if I would be willing to talk about being the park Santa next year. I tried to avoid jumping up and down and screaming, "Yes! Yes! Yes!"

It was February when they called. The hours were right. They let people take their own pictures and videos. I was very quick to say yes.

It would be the Friday after Thanksgiving, almost a year away, before I would assume the role, but I immediately began to tell people that I was the Santa at Stone Mountain Park.

It was a dream come true.

The park had a tremendous holiday celebration with many activities and programs in which I would take part—and the holiday celebration always began with a grand opening on the Friday night after Thanksgiving. It took place (and still does) on the lawn of the park that runs from the base of the mountain, up a long slope, to Memorial Hall at the top of a hill. Thousands of people arrayed themselves around the lawn to watch the festivities, which included music, choir concerts, Santa's grand entrance, and then a special Christmas laser show.

That year, my first, the Stone Mountain crew decided I would ride in on a horse-drawn carriage. They brought in one of the carriages that take folks on tours of the park, and it was beautiful. But it also obscured Santa from the kids' view. It was impossible for folks sitting on the lawn to see the carriage and me unless they were sitting at the top of a steep bank. As the carriage made its way along the road, some of the kids from near the bank began to come down to get closer. Then, suddenly, one lost his footing and began to slide down. I could just imagine his leg going under the wheel and getting broken. I was screaming at the driver to stop, but the noise of the music and the people screaming drowned me out.

The boy slid right down the bank and missed the rear wheel by inches. I began planning for the next year right then and there. No carriages.

The next year Santa was to ride in a golf cart down the lawn and through the crowd of thousands for the laser show. There would be one cart for Santa and one for Mrs. Claus, both decorated with hundreds of tiny lights and a borrowed blue light from the police department. But who ever heard of Santa and Mrs. Claus driving golf carts, right? We decided a policeman would drive me into the crowd, and Sue would drive my Annie.

the ℛed Suit Diaries

It was a bitter cold evening as we made our way from the police area to the top of the lawn. The chill didn't keep away the people though; they were there in droves. After a wait for our cue, we were off. The policeman turned on the lights, at which time we made a serious discovery. When a blue light is on the front of a golf cart, there is no way you can see past it, except for that brief moment when the light revolves just past your face.

We started down the center of the lawn, trying to dodge the people we couldn't see. Annie and Sue were right behind us. Then we found that if we leaned out the side of the cart, we could almost see around the light. So there we went, Santa leaning out one side and a fuzz person leaning out the other as we made our way down the lawn.

Going slowly was a given—we were creeping along, and it was easy for the people to come up to the cart to shake hands or relay messages. We were going so slowly they could have read *War and Peace* to me!

Soon we were all but mobbed by the people. The cold was forgotten, the light was forgotten, and I was having a ball responding to the crowd.

I looked back at Annie, who was in her element too, kids all around her. I remember thinking how beautiful she looked in her outfit and how proud I was that she was my Mrs. Claus.

Meanwhile, the policeman was trying to get people to move so we could go on and the laser show could begin. Eventually the crowd parted, and we made our way to the railroad station where the Santa set was located.

Maybe golf carts weren't the answer either. Wait till next year.

Suddenly Christmas was here again. (It never ceases to amaze me how quickly those months between Santa stuff pass.) So then it was the next grand opening, and this time we decided to try a fire truck.

We would have to go down that same road again at the front of the lawn, but I would get up on top of the truck. I would be up much higher than I had been in the carriage, and the kids couldn't get to me so they wouldn't run down the bank toward the fire truck.

Yeah, sure! Another great idea down the drain.

The truck showed up on time, and I chatted with the firefighters while we waited for our cue. They told

the Red Suit Diaries

me they had just washed and polished the truck. It looked clean and shiny.

When it was time to go, I climbed up to the highest flat place and straddled the thing. Oops! The firefighters had done a great job polishing the truck, but they had forgotten to dry off the puddle on the top. So I just did it for them. That was cold water too, you can believe.

But the trip down the road went smoothly; I was up so high and so far away from the people that no one could see my teeth chattering behind my smile. The truck did not intimidate the kids on the bank though, and down they went. Now, instead of a flimsy carriage wheel breaking a leg, I had to worry about a dual-wheeled fire truck crushing a leg beyond repair!

Then a moment of terror—a boy of about six fell and started to tumble down the bank. Just as I was about to look away to avoid seeing the carnage, a girl of about twelve, maybe his big sister, reached out, grabbed his arm, and stopped him in midflight. She dug in her heels, and they stopped before they reached the bottom of the bank.

Dreams

Merry Christmas, Santa, and thank you, Lord! Sue and I agreed that the next year we'd leave wheels out of our plans.

This time we found a way to use all of the above. I would ride in a quiet police car to the house where the laser show projectors were located. Before the show, the house is flush with the lawn surface. Just before the show it rises out of the ground and positions itself above the lawn.

The plan was that I would go into the house and ride it up while standing in front of a glass wall. Then as soon as we stopped rising I would step out of a glass door onto a concrete apron and greet the people along the front of the lawn as I made my way, walking, over to the train station.

It was a great plan, with only one glitch. I rode up as the spotlights were on me, I was waving through the glass, and it was wonderful. (Annie's dad videotaped it. It did look great.) Then, the glitch.

When the thing stopped I reached for the door and pushed. It didn't move. I pushed again and again and was about to panic when one of the laser crew guys shouted, "Pull!"

the Red Suit Diaries

I pulled and felt a rush of cool air as it opened. The spotlights were on me, and the videotape clearly shows the panic on my face when the door wouldn't open.

I stepped onto the apron and began to wave to the crowd. I obliged as many as I could until the spotlight went out, the signal for me to get out of the way and let the laser show begin.

It's the beaming smiles of the children though—not the flash of camera lights or entertaining lasers—that shine in my dreams.

Meet Santa's Elves

One of the most charming things about my Santa duty at Stone Mountain Park is the elves whom I work alongside every night.

Before my first night I had been told that there would be some little people there as elves, and this had intrigued me. But by the time the season rolled around, I had forgotten that they were to be there.

That night, I finally made it to the railway station after my ride on the carriage and my struggle through the mob scene. I walked into the chicken restaurant inside the station and immediately wished I had run a reconnaissance of the place before the first night.

The Santa throne was set on a platform about six inches off the floor. (All the better for kids to fall off onto a ceramic tile floor.) But, horror of horrors, there was no cushion on the throne. The chair was a plain plywood seat that was precisely level with the floor. There was no way my backside would be able to take four hours of sitting on this thing as kids climbed all over my lap.

Before I even sat down, I told Sue Stoll, the special events person on duty, that I would need a cushion. She went all the way home to get one that would do for the night, and for the next night I planned on bringing a special wheelchair-type cushion that would get me through the season.

I didn't really notice the little people elves while all this was going on, then suddenly there they were. I'd never met them before, but to the kids in line we had to look like we'd been acquainted for a long, long time. We passed a casual yet very friendly hello, like old buddies, and over the next four hours, in the brief moments between kids, we got better acquainted.

the R̄ed Suit Diaries

I learned that they were brother and sister, part of a large family of little people that lived in Ellenwood, southeast of Atlanta. There was also a large extended family of little people, and over the years I would meet many of them as they cycled in and out of work as elves at the park. Trent was sixteen and Heidi was eighteen. They were not only cute little elves but terrific young people. Their parents, Mary Alice and Pete, were particularly fun. They had been elves a lot longer than I had been Santa, and I learned a lot from both of them.

I was so very impressed with the loving way they related to the kids, to me, and to each other. They would show me, with their smiles and graciousness in response to the variety of ways they were treated for their size, how to be a big person on the inside.

The making of dreams, you see, can be delivered in all shapes and sizes.

Santa in the Spotlight

Andy Warhol is reputed to have said that every person is entitled to fifteen minutes of fame. I don't think he said it would come in two-minute increments.

But, then again, who can complain when that fame is so positive?

In March of 1992 there was an article about FODA in the *Atlanta Journal-Constitution*. The article had several results. There was an immediate increase in the amount of people coming to FODA for help, and there was an increase in the number of people and companies donating equipment and money. But it didn't stop there.

Early in December of 1992 the Atlanta bureau chief of *NBC Nightly News* with Tom Brokaw called the house and told Annie that he wanted to do a story about the Santa who gave away wheelchairs. I was out doing a Santa gig at the time, but Annie didn't hesitate to tell him we would do it!

The next day I returned the call and spoke to Dave Riggs, the bureau chief. I learned that he had a son with cerebral palsy and that he had written our names in his "futures book" when he had read the article in March. *Good grief,* I thought, *the media really does have power.* Boy, was I about to find out just how true that was!

We scheduled a time for his crew to come to FODA and film there, and also a time for them to meet me at

Stone Mountain Park for more filming. We would do the park part before my scheduled start time of 6:00 P.M. so we wouldn't upset any of the folks in line.

I decided to wear a red shirt for the workshop filming instead of my normal navy blue FODA "uniform" shirt. Since I had done some television production while I was in the Marine Corps and had been on local television a couple of times, I knew what to expect and was not particularly intimidated. At least I wasn't until Bob Dotson walked into the room.

Bob and his pieces about people and places around the country had been favorites of mine for a long time. I couldn't believe he was going to be interviewing me.

But I was prepared. I had brought in a ringer to be the star of this segment. His name was Ryan Mercer, a delightful youngster with cerebral palsy. I just knew that Ryan would be his charming self and steal the show. And he did.

I decided that I wanted a ringer for the park segments too, so I called the parents of three of my favorite kids. Jeff and Kathy Shoppe's daughters, Lindsey, six, Stevie, four, and Mindy, two and a half, were delightful. They had wonderful personalities, and they were true believers in the one true Santa.

When I walked out of the kitchen of the chicken restaurant that Friday night, I couldn't believe my eyes. The place was packed. There, all set up, was the film crew, Bob Dotson, Jeff and Kathy and their girls, Ryan Mercer, and his mom and dad. The line to see Santa was full, and the restaurant was packed with people eating the delicious fried chicken. Well, so much for having a private time for the filming.

I didn't want to risk losing the moment with the Shoppe girls, so I ignored them. I did tell Jeff and Kathy what I was doing so they wouldn't wonder what was happening. They knew how much I cared for their kids, and my ignoring them would be a surprise. I just didn't want them to lose any of the spontaneity for that brief moment of the interview.

I sat down on my throne and let the sound guys hook up their microphones and watched the camera guy get into position. Then I motioned the girls to come see me.

I did all the welcoming things while I positioned Mindy and Stevie on my left leg and Lindsey on my right. Cameras were rolling. I decided to start with Lindsey. Sometimes the littlest kid will echo every item the older ones ask for, and I knew that would be some absolutely charming footage.

Preliminaries over, I asked the question, "Tell me what you would like to have for Christmas. You first, Lindsey."

"OK," she said. "I want a bike."

Immediately, explosively, a wee voice on my left leg said, "I want a bike too!"

I turned and looked at Mindy. "You want a bike too?" I asked.

She nodded. I turned back to Lindsey expectantly.

"I want some Barbies," Lindsey responded.

Again, Mindy, "I want some Barbies too."

Again I turned and asked, "You want some Barbies too?" She nodded again.

Lindsey had one more item. Mindy echoed that one too. I looked at Lindsey and Stevie and said, "I think we have an echo in here, don't we?" Then I turned to Stevie. She had three items on her list, and Mindy echoed each one of them.

I looked at Lindsey and Stevie again and said, "We really do have an echo in here, don't we?" They both nodded very emphatically.

I turned to Mindy again. "Is there anything else you want for Christmas, Mindy?" She shook her head no. She would be happy just getting everything her big sisters had on their lists.

I knew that NBC had some of the cutest footage they could ever hope to get, but we went ahead and did another segment with Ryan and a couple of other kids.

Nothing came close to what we already had. I began to get very excited about how all this film would be edited together. The way I saw it, they should have enough good stuff to use for the entire half hour of a nightly news show!

Dave Riggs called the next day and said everything looked great, and that they were editing it and hoping to "feed" it to New York that afternoon. He promised to let me know when it would run.

It was a long wait those several days. Then he called on the morning of the twenty-third. It was scheduled to run as the last segment that night. RATS!!! I had a

92

Santa gig that evening in Sandy Springs. A big-time advertising executive was having a party for his staff, and I was part of the entertainment. No telling where I would be at 6:27 P.M.

Annie and I called a few folks, and we set up the VCR. Then I went to the party, which was in a huge, plush house. The host asked if I would come into another room and talk with each kid while seated in a nice Queen Anne chair. I agreed and started to work my way through the little ones.

Then I noticed that there was a screen in front of me that was almost the size of a drive-in movie screen. All of a sudden it hit me that it was a television! I pulled up my sleeve and looked at my watch. Mickey's little hand was on the six, and his big hand was on the five! At that moment the host walked by, and I leaned between the two girls on my lap and grabbed him. I told him to turn on the TV to channel 11, the local NBC affiliate.

It was on a commercial first, and then there was Tom Brokaw saying something I couldn't hear. But I could see a graphic of a red sleeve, white fur, and a hand with a white glove holding a pair of pliers. Then there was my face!

Our host looked at the TV, then looked at me and started yelling, "Hey, it's our Santa! Hey, everybody, our Santa is on Brokaw!"

The room filled up immediately as I sat enthralled, watching what many millions of people around the country were seeing. I couldn't hear a word that was said, but it looked as sweet as it had during the filming. I was dying to hear the whole thing.

As soon as I finished with the kids, I went in to where the adults were and answered a thousand questions about how the NBC thing had happened. These were advertising people, and many of them told me how much those two minutes of prime-time news probably cost. I wasn't interested in that; I just wanted to know what the impact on our ministry would be.

How many people would call in that we could help? Would there be so many we couldn't help any of them? Would there be any financial support that could enable us to help all those folks?

As soon as I could, I slipped out the door and started for home. I called home on the cell phone and asked Annie how it was. "Fantastic!" she bubbled. "The phone started to ring before it was even on." (It had been broadcast earlier in some markets, apparently.) I began to wonder how they had found us so fast.

I walked into the house, peeling off my Santa coat, and heard Annie on the phone. I grabbed the VCR remote and started trying to find the right spot on the tape. Annie finished that call and said, "That was number twenty-four. It came from Miami. You can get the rest of them."

Immediately, it rang again. And it kept ringing immediately after the previous call was finished for the next two hours, most of the next day, and many times more over the next week.

We also started to get mail. A lot of it had cryptic addresses such as, "Wheelchair Santa, Stone Mountain, Georgia." One was addressed, "Santa who makes wheelchairs, Stone Mountain, North Carolina"! I don't know how many we might've missed, but we got over one hundred letters from all over the country.

Charlie, our mailman, knew us and knew about our wheelchair ministry, and he made sure any odd letters that made it to the Stone Mountain post office also made it to our house. Many people sent checks. Some still do, even years later. We've had items shipped in from all over the country, and we've shipped stuff everywhere as well.

People even came up to us in restaurants and in grocery stores and said they had seen us on TV.

It was a heady experience. I tried to keep it in perspective and give all the glory to the One who made it all possible. I still take every opportunity to make sure people find out that I am just a sinner saved by God's grace and called to serve in a ministry much bigger than myself.

Without God's involvement in our ministry and our lives, we are truly nothing. My prayer is that the love that Bob Dotson said was shown in my life is taken for what it is—the reflected love of our Lord and Savior, Jesus Christ.

After two years at Gwinnett Place Mall I wanted a new place for the season of 1991. I would be at Stone Mountain Park on the weekends from 6:00 to 9:00 P.M. so I had all day to spend somewhere else.

I called a friend from church who was a professional photographer. Dan Gunn would make a great Santa himself if his beard was white instead of coal black. He is certainly built for the part. He is also a superb portrait and wedding photographer. He and I had talked about taking pictures somewhere, and now was our chance to do something together. He contacted the manager of a huge store in Stone Mountain called American Fare, which was owned by Kmart.

The manager said he would provide a place for us if we would cover all the expenses of staffing and equipping the set. We agreed. Dan took care of all the details. I just had to show up at the appointed time in my red suit. Piece of cake.

Well, from the beginning, the staff and I were about the only ones who did show up. There weren't big crowds at the American Fare store, so Dan and I decided during the first week just to relax and have a good time. We cut back on our staff and began to enjoy precious moments like these.

She looked like a little doll as she ran toward our set. Her two-year-old legs were churning, her brown curls were bouncing, and her arms were pumping as she came closer and closer. She got to the top of the ramp and was just six feet away when she suddenly slammed on the brakes. She looked me in the face, and her big smile slowly faded away. Then she whirled and was down the ramp in a flash, running to her mother's side.

Mom walked up to the side of the stage. "I'm sorry," she said.

"I'm not," I reassured her. "A lot of kids do that. Keep bringing her back. She'll run right up here and jump in my lap eventually."

"OK, we'll be back," Mom said, smiling.

The next day she was back, and here came her little one again. Right to the top of the ramp, one quick look, and away she went.

the $\mathcal{R}$ed Suit Diaries

Mom came up again and said she just didn't know what had come over her little girl. "She's always been so friendly to everyone."

"Sure," I said with a laugh. "How many of them had a white beard and were wearing a red suit?"

Mom laughed.

"Just keep coming, she'll be fine," I said.

For four days more they came, and each time the scene was a rerun. It was almost like rewinding a VCR. Then I told Mom I would be at Stone Mountain that night and that she could bring her baby there too.

She did. I saw them in the line, and from the look of delighted expectancy on the little one's face, I was sure that this time would be the charm.

But nooo! As soon as it was her turn she did a turn of her own and dashed out the exit into her daddy's arms. I saw her shake her head and knew what her dad had asked her. She certainly didn't want to go see that guy!

The next day at American Fare, here she came again, running for the ramp. This time she got to the top of the ramp and didn't stop! She ran right up to me as I put out my arms, and she ran right into them, smiling all the way.

I couldn't believe it! I sat her up on my lap, and we nearly had an adult conversation. She told me she had been a good girl, told me all the ways she had been good, and then told me everything that was on her list for Christmas.

Dan took some pictures and a video. I thanked the little girl for coming and set her on the floor, and away she went in that familiar running style. I looked at Mom and saw that she had sprung a leak in her face. She wasn't the only one.

That was to be my only year at American Fare. I thought I might see the little one again at Stone Mountain Park the next year, but she was a no-show. It would be a while before we would meet again.

It was 1995, four years later, when I had a delightful conversation with a six-year-old little lady at the park. When she got back on the floor, she ran to her mother, and I realized it was the same mom from four years before.

I called her over and said it was good to see her. She told me that her family had moved away for four years and now was back, and her daughter had insisted that she be taken to the park to see "her Santa Claus."

Mom told me that her little girl absolutely loved Santa and had the pictures from American Fare on her bedroom wall. I was so thrilled to learn how this little one felt about me.

She had felt the love of Christ I was trying so hard to emulate. It meant so much to me, and my prayer was that all the other kids who had been on my lap had felt some of that love too.

Sometimes, showing that love has to take a direct approach.

A family of five kids came dashing up the ramp one day as Mom waited and watched. From the look of them, it was obvious that money was a problem. Their clothes were clean but very worn, and the kids, boys and girls, all needed haircuts. The oldest was a girl of around twelve, the youngest a boy of around three. They were healthy, active children, and I could see this mom had her hands full!

I wanted to start with the oldest, but as soon as I turned to her she said she wanted to be last. So I started with the youngest. All of them had routine things on their lists, and the interviews proceeded smoothly.

As each of the kids finished their lists, the older one grabbed them off my lap and sent them on their way to Mom. Then it was her turn. She sat on my lap and looked me straight in the face.

"Santa," she said seriously, "all I really want for Christmas is for us to have a Christmas tree. Mom said that there isn't enough money since Daddy ran off for us to have a tree, much less presents. But I just want us to have a tree at least. The little kids at least deserve a tree!"

I didn't know what to say, really. But I found some words flowing out. "Christmas is a time when dreams do come true. Don't give up on yours yet." I gave her a gentle hug and nudged her on her way.

As she went down the ramp, Dan took the videotape of our interview out of the camcorder and headed over to the VCR to show it to the excited family that was gathered around the TV. He looked at me, and I gave him our signal that meant he was to give the tape for free. I watched as the kids watched themselves, enchanted.

Mom stood behind them, nodding her head gently as the tears flowed. When the tape ended she started to walk away, but Dan called to her and handed her the tape, saying, "Santa wanted you to have this." She grabbed it, clutched it to her heart, and turned to look at me. I smiled and waved. She nodded and walked away, her head down.

Dan walked up to the edge of the stage and said, "Tell me about this one, Santa." I related what the oldest girl had told me. He said quietly, "Well, what do you say we buy them a Christmas tree?"

"Great idea!" I responded. He nodded and walked toward the sales floor.

In a few minutes I heard a shriek echoing through the store. That sound was followed closely by several smaller shrieks and screams, a total of six screamers the way it sounded to me. Since no one was in line to see Santa, I decided to take a break and walk down to the bottom of the ramp. Dan came back, and I said, "What did you do?"

He shrugged and said, "I gave them a hundred dollar bill."

"Good," I responded. "We'll split it."

"No way," he answered. "This time I get to be Santa Claus."

We were chatting away a few minutes later when I heard the sound of running footsteps headed in our direction. I turned around just in time to be nearly knocked off my feet by five hurtling bodies. They were shouting, "Thank you, Santa! Thank you! Thank you! Thank you!" They were hugging me from my knees to my shoulders, and all were laughing and crying at the same time.

Then I saw Mom pushing the grocery cart our way. Tears were streaming down her face. She stopped the cart, walked boldly up to me, and threw her arms around my neck. Her body was shaking from the sobbing. She managed to say, "Thank you so very much. I believe, I believe!" Then she turned me loose and headed for the door with her cart.

I turned to look at our crew. The girls were crying, and I even saw a gleam in Dan's eye. I walked up to

the Red Suit Diaries

him and said quietly, "You got to be Santa Claus, but I got all the credit."

He said, "Yeah, and that is just the way I wanted it to be."

Didn't I tell you he'd make a great Santa?

The Dangers of Decongestant

One of the great fears of being Santa is that you will get sick or hurt and not be able to make your shift. But since hundreds of kids crawl across Santa's lap, and there's no telling what kinds of communicable diseases they bring with them, it seems inevitable that you'll catch something.

This has only happened to me once. Well, I didn't actually miss my shift (but maybe I should have!). One morning I woke up feeling rotten. I didn't have a fever, but I did have a runny nose and teary eyes and just felt terrible. I took a couple of aspirin and a twenty-four-hour decongestant.

It didn't help much, so a couple of hours later I took another eight-hour decongestant. After all, I didn't want my nose dripping onto some kid's lap!

Annie wanted me to stay home, but I just couldn't. We weren't drawing much of a crowd at American Fare, but I didn't like to think of even one kid being disappointed.

I was OK when I got to the store. My nose had stopped running, and I felt much improved. Then about two hours into the day, I began to get drowsy. It wasn't long before I could barely hold my head up.

I took a break and went for a walk around the set. Didn't help. I went over to the Taco Bell stand and got a Diet Coke. Didn't help. I shoulda had a Coke with sugar in it. I went and got one. Didn't help.

When the kids came, it was all I could do to stay awake enough to make sense to them. And as soon as he finished taking the pictures, Dan would walk to the edge of the stage. If he saw I was about to close my eyes, he would slap the floor to keep me awake. Eventually I made him quit taking videos. I was afraid some parent would take it home and, under close examination, conclude that Santa was drunk!

I felt like my shift would never end. In fact, I spent the last couple of hours just being glad I didn't have to go from there to Stone Mountain Park for an evening shift.

When my day was finally done, I managed to make it to the storeroom and then out the back door to my car. I was scared to death I would fall asleep at the wheel, so I turned off the heater and opened the window. The nippy air did the trick, and I made it home safely.

Soon there were red clothes all along the hall and up the stairs, and in a few moments I was sound asleep. It was 5:30 in the afternoon. But you guessed it! I snapped wide awake at 4:30 in the morning, and I couldn't go back to sleep. After an hour of tossing and turning, I finally got up and went down to the living room to read the paper. That's where Annie found me the next morning at 8:30, sound asleep in the recliner with the paper in my lap.

I did learn a valuable lesson though. There is a limit to how much decongestant a person should take at one time. Unless he wants to take a long nap, that is.

Oh, the perils of being Santa!

The Naughty and the Nice

I'm sure a lot of people have secret fantasies of being "discovered" by a Hollywood director and becoming rich and famous. I was sure that I would be called to appear in the remake of *Miracle on 34th Street*. Didn't happen. Surely I could make it into *Ernest Saves Christmas*. Missed again. Then I did get a call.

One year, the *Atlanta Journal-Constitution* ran a story about the FODA ministry and included a picture of me. Soon after, I got a call from a company named DHR, Inc., which sold gifts from the Atlanta Gift Mart.

It seemed they had a Christmas gift show there every year, in July, and they thought it would be a great promotional idea to have Santa in their shop for the show. They also wanted to feature me in a full-page ad for their annual show guide. I thought it would be a lot of fun to have a few days of only adults coming to sit on Santa's lap. So I agreed.

DHR called back and told me to go to a certain professional photographer for an appointment for the photo shoot. A few days later they called to say the pictures were perfect, and that they'd had a hard time choosing just one for the ad. They promised to save me some copies of the guide and told me they would see me on the first day of the show, which was about two months away.

When July rolled around, it felt a bit weird putting on my red suit, especially in the middle of an Atlanta summer. The maintenance crew at the Gift Mart did a few double takes themselves when I got out of the van and started for the service elevators. By now I was used to double takes regardless of what I was wearing, but I did feel just a little more conspicuous in my full regalia. (By the way, that full regalia is the most expensive suit of clothes I have ever owned. From boots to hat it is worth almost six hundred dollars! That's more than my fanciest Marine Corps officer dress uniform.)

I had taken my throne down there a couple of days earlier, so I knew where I was going. But I wasn't entirely prepared to open the doors and walk out into a crowd of adults, mostly women, all with Christmas on their minds. At least, that's what I thought they had on their minds.

DHR wanted to give each buyer a picture of themselves sitting on Santa's lap. That seemed like a good idea to me at the time, but I hadn't factored into the equation the effect that the open bar would have on the buyers and their reaction to sitting on the lap of that right jolly old elf.

We started with the pictures right away each of the three days, and all proceeded well at first. But as each day wore on, I became aware that the women were becoming more and more friendly.

I decided on the second day that I would take Annie along for protection. She didn't dress in her Mrs. Claus outfit but made sure that people knew who she was. Unfortunately, she decided to take a walk around the Mart for a while, and I was left alone.

In the parade of women going by, one of them threw herself across my lap, grabbed my left hand, placed it on her hip, and leaned back for the picture. Then she said in a low, suggestive voice, "You are about the cutest thing I have ever seen. Are you staying in a hotel in Atlanta?"

"No," I answered tentatively. "I live here, in Stone Mountain."

110

"Well," she responded, "I was kind of hoping you might be interested in this." She opened her right hand and dangled a hotel room key in my face.

"Good grief, no!" I stammered. "Mrs. Claus and I already have plans for the evening."

"Oh, well," she said. "More's the pity. Well, you can't blame a girl for asking, can you?" And she eased herself off my lap and wandered on.

I couldn't believe it! Santa had been hit on! What was this world coming to?

Later I did get an invitation that was more appealing. A woman sat down primly, posed politely, and then asked me if I would consider going to High Point, North Carolina, and being the Santa at her gift shop. Since High Point is adjacent to Greensboro, where I was raised and where some of my relatives were still living, I gave her my FODA business card and told her to give me a call. She did a few days later. (You will read about High Point later on.)

Another buyer asked if I would like to go to Lake City, South Carolina, and she made it so appealing I agreed to talk to her too. (This is also covered later.)

Well, it was a very interesting few days at DHR. We took a total of 555 photos. And there were no children and only six or eight men.

But there were plenty of women. I remember one Jewish woman who said, "I hope my rabbi doesn't hear about this!"

"Don't worry," I promised. "I won't tell him!"

"Oh, but I will!" she answered with a wicked cackle.

There's one more thing I remember about those ladies. The women who were average size all worried about whether they were too heavy for Santa. Those of more ample size simply sat down, with a lot of giggles, and didn't seem to care whether they were too heavy or not.

What they didn't know and what I was not about to tell them was that I much preferred the women with plenty of padding rather than the skinny ones who could perform surgery on my leg by squirming around with their sharp bones.

As long as I have my shin bone perfectly vertical and my thigh bone perfectly horizontal, weight is not a problem. It's the bony posteriors that will kill a Santa, and this crowd had a bunch of them.

Childlike Faith

Dear Santa,

i am 5 years old and I beleeve in you. do you have a carrot garden? how many carrots do you feed your raindeer? HOW did you meet Mrs. Claus? thank you for my presents. Next time you bring me a present i'll have a plate of cookies for you. What kind do you like? i like star ones with sprinkles on top. can when you fly in your sleigh, can you touch the stars for real? i love you Santa Claus and Missis Claus,

from, SPENCER, age 5

Quadruplets

One of the mysteries of being Santa is what makes one child climb right up onto Santa's lap and talk his head off, and another child, same age, same everything, stop within arms' reach and pitch a hissy fit of screaming and kicking.

It's become clear that most of the screamers are between eleven months and three years of age; there is little else to categorize them. But after I'd had about 75,000 kids on my lap, I developed some theories.

First of all, I believe parental influence has a profound effect. Some parents tell their kids that Santa is a warm and loving figure who would never hurt them. Other parents use Santa as a disciplinary club. "If you don't behave, I'm going to tell Santa on you." Have you ever said that? Be careful, I know if you have. (Remember, Santa knows everything!) And some parents use Santa as a powerful, vengeful, even mean figure. "Santa is going to get you for that!"

I remember one little girl who looked me in the face and asked if I was going to put pepper in her eyes. I said, "Good grief, no, of course not. Who told you that?"

She shrugged and answered, "My mama told me if I didn't go to sleep right away on Christmas night, then Santa would come and put pepper in my eyes."

Can you believe that? I couldn't either.

I hugged her and said, "No, baby, Santa would never do anything to hurt you and certainly would never put pepper in your eyes. Santa loves you very much." I wanted this child to know the truth! I wanted her to feel love from me. That feeling would overpower the mere words of her mama.

After all my research I have found some parallels to this situation. You see, the way children develop their concept of Santa is not unlike the way people develop their concept of God. Some preachers portray God as a loving, forgiving, welcoming, grace-filled father figure. Others tell their congregations that God is a vengeful, punishing figure.

The lives of many people are damaged because they are taught that God is "going to get them." They are never taught how to develop a close relationship with a loving Lord. Jesus said, "I am the way, the truth, and the life." I want the love I feel for each of these kids, and the adults too, to reflect that truth.

So what really causes a screamer? Well, I believe we have to ask the age-old question: What is more important, heredity or environment? Are screamers born that way or are they created by their family situation?

I mulled over that question for years, and then one night at Stone Mountain Park I was given the perfect opportunity for an answer. A family brought their quadruplets to see me!

It happened suddenly and caught me off guard. A mother brought up a little girl about a year old and sat her on my lap. The child looked at me, smiled, and started fiddling with my beard. I watched her intently. Then I became aware that a crowd had gathered at my feet.

Trent was the elf that night, and he nudged me in the arm and said, "Santa, look at this." I looked and saw that arrayed around the floor right in front of me was a mom, a dad, and three more little girls who were dead ringers for the one on my lap. Startled, I blurted out, "Good grief, there are four of them! It's a litter!"

Mom laughed and started to hand me the one on her lap. The little one immediately started to scream. Mom withdrew that attempt. Dad had two more of them. One was sound asleep, the other was eyeing me warily. Dad started to put the awake one on my lap, and she grabbed him so tightly around the neck I expected him to become purple in the face. He leaned back, and she loosened her grip just enough for him to hand me the sleeper.

Then he and Mom slid back to my feet and held their beautiful little ones on their laps while two of the proudest grandparents you would ever see took at least a roll each of pictures and then ground away with a camcorder for what seemed like ten minutes. But it didn't bother me—I was relishing every moment.

Then, too soon, Mom and Dad struggled to their feet, and Gramps and Grammy came and got the two on my lap. I had time for a brief question or two, but the answers were lost to time and confusion. I don't remember where they were from or who they were, but I will never forget that beautiful face that looked so adoringly at me. And that was only one of them!

OK, let's review this now. One of the four was friendly and interested, one was sound asleep, apparently unimpressed, one was afraid but not out of control, and one was absolutely terrified.

So now, what about that old question, the heredity/ environment thing? These kids were genetically identical (or at least extremely close to identical for you geneticists). They had the same environment, same parents, same house, and same grandparents.

Well, it soon became obvious to me that there was no answer to that question. I made up my mind to quit looking and just relax and enjoy the kids, from the sleepers to the screamers. They all need love, and they need to feel love from Santa.

I guarantee they will get that from this Santa for sure.

A Cry for Help

The interesting thing about asking for faith from children is that you end up having to develop your own. And mine was tested by a boy I saw in line one day. I thought he looked a bit older than most of the kids I was seeing, and then I noticed he looked sad. Before he even approached me I knew this was going to be a different interview.

He waited politely until the girl on my lap was finished, but he as much as pushed his way past her as soon as her feet hit the floor. I looked around for a parent but didn't see any likely candidates.

The moment he sat down, I was struck by his over-powering smell. There was no doubt he had come to the mall with a smoker in a closed-up vehicle. I thought immediately (as I always do) of what his lungs must look like with all that smoke in them. But there was something more to the odor. There was sweat, burned motor oil, wet dog, and wet fireplace mixed in various degrees.

I looked closely at him and saw several small bruises on his neck and cheek, like he had been pinched

the R̃ed Suit Diaries

firmly. His blond hair was unkempt and dirty. His three-tone tan coat was grimy too, and I could see evidence of all the odors on the too-small coat.

There was an intensity about him that was unsettling. I looked into pale blue eyes that held a deep sadness, and I became uneasy before I had even had a chance to speak.

I was about to open my mouth when he reached across my face and pulled me close. Normally I would have taken that gesture as an attempt to pull my beard, and I would have grabbed his hand. This time I didn't move.

He thrust his mouth toward my ear and whispered, "Santa, there is only one thing I want for Christmas. Only one thing."

I moved away from him and, looking into those eyes again, said, "And what would that be?"

He pulled me back again and whispered, "All I want for Christmas is for my dad to stop beating me." He said it in a flat voice, devoid of emotion, as if he was stating a fact that Santa should already have been aware of.

There must have been an audible hissing sound as the air went out of me. I felt a sinking in the pit of my stomach. I don't know that I have ever felt so helpless in my life.

In desperation I looked around to see if there was anyone nearby who could help me deal with what I had just heard. A policeman, a social worker, anybody! But no one had heard this plea but me.

Then I saw him.

Standing by the exit, lounging casually against a post, was a man who immediately reminded me of a snake. He had on dirty blue jeans and a blue jean jacket. His baseball cap had an ad for Caterpillar tractors on it. He had long, stringy, dirty black hair and was smoking in defiance of the mall rule.

But worst of all were the eyes. They were beady and burning with an intense hatred—of me, of the boy, and I think of society in general. He stood there so arrogantly, thinking he was all that a man ought to be, so macho, so masculine, so tough, and all he really was, was sick. He was so sick he should have been institutionalized!

More than anything, I wanted to be the one to make that happen. But how? What could I do? What could I say?

The boy's sad face was looking at me so expectantly, waiting for me to make his Christmas—his lifetime—wish come true. Very slowly he opened up his fists. As they opened like a morning glory, I saw that the palms of his hands were covered with scars, scars on top of scars. Someone, no doubt the snake, had been using this child's palms as ashtrays. I tried to control my revulsion and anger.

If the snake knew his boy had told me all this, there was no telling what he might do. I had to be careful not to aggravate the situation if I couldn't find a solution. And there was no way I could solve this horrifying problem.

I drew the boy as close as I could and spoke quietly into his ear. "Oh, son, I would give anything if I could make your request come true, I really would. Do you go to school?" I asked.

He nodded very slowly.

I pulled him close again. "I will promise you something," I said. "This won't go on forever. Someday you're going to be grown up enough, and this will stop. I also promise you that Santa loves you and wants this to stop. But, more importantly, God loves you too. He wants this to stop. And someday your dad is going to have to account for his treatment of you.

"Now there is something I want you to do for me. I want you to tell your favorite teacher what you told me. And I want you to show her your hands and your neck. OK?"

He nodded slowly, and his blue eyes seemed to have a bit more sparkle in them.

Then I nudged him off my lap and stood him between my legs. I reached out and enfolded him in my arms. He buried his face in my beard.

I whispered in his ear. "Remember, God loves you, and I love you too," I was able to say through a very constricted throat. Then I turned him loose. He stepped back, smiled slightly, and turned and walked slowly toward the snake.

They walked over to the elevator at the bottom of the exit ramp and rode to the upper level. I watched as they walked away. Just before they went out of sight, the little guy turned around, waved, smiled, and blew me a kiss.

I said quietly, "Please, Lord, take care of him."

"Huh?" said the little girl now on my lap.

I looked her in the face, smiled broadly, and said, "Hello!"

Jolly Old Saint Nick was back from the pain.

Well, no, not really. That pain still won't go away, even all these years later.

Birthday Boy

Hardly a shift on the throne goes by that some kid doesn't say to me that it's his or her birthday. If I have the time, I try to sing the birthday song, and, as you would hear from Annie, that's not really a gift! But birthdays are a lot of fun, and sometimes they develop into something really special.

Like the time I met a lovely young woman who had waited in line all by herself. When it was her turn she came to me and said, "I really need to talk to you. Would you please call me?" She handed me a slip of paper with a phone number on it.

This wasn't the first time I'd been asked about doing other appearances. Besides, I'd joke on occasions like this, she might be a Hollywood scout or a casting director for a movie.

When I called the next morning, she told me her son's fifth birthday was coming up and that she wanted to have Santa show up at the party. I agreed, and it was a routine party, really. Very quickly the kids got bored with Santa and the adults got interested. I stood at the amply loaded table of goodies, stuffing my face and telling a few of my stories before leaving.

The next year the mom called me again and invited me to her son's party. The family had moved to Marietta, miles away, but I agreed to go again. The crowd was mostly the new neighbors, so I had a new audience. Same result: good time, good food, good company. I figured that was the end of it. The little guy had a new sister, and he was about to grow out of Santa Claus.

But, surprise, she called me again the next year. This time she didn't want me to come to a party. She had another problem. She told me her little guy was not convinced Santa was real, because his friends had told him there was a different Santa everywhere you go. So she wanted my entire schedule for any appearances I would be making during the season. I gave it to her as accurately as I could, including every "one-night stand" that would involve a public appearance.

I was doing a Saturday afternoon appearance at a grocery store for a radio station, and Mom apparently did her grocery shopping there. I recognized her son and called him over to my lap for a visit. I could tell he was skeptical.

I was at the American Fare store, and Mom drove clear across Atlanta to shop there one Saturday. I called him again to my lap.

I was at Stone Mountain Park the next weekend, and sure enough there they were. Another quick visit. And this time he was less skeptical.

On another occasion, I arrived on a motorcycle for a tree-lighting ceremony. When I got out of the motorcycle sidecar, there they were again, smiling and waving. I waved back. He looked almost convinced.

The next weekend he and Mom were driving down a road when a fire truck pulled out of a side street right in front of them—and, lo and behold, there was Santa riding on the top of the truck. Santa turned around, looked directly into the car, and waved.

I could see the boy's mental crank turning. *It looks like . . . could it be . . . yes, it is! Santa!*

The fire truck turned into a shopping center, made a couple of passes through the parking lot, then stopped along the curb near some stores. After making my way through a small crowd that had gathered, I went into a fancy toy shop, and guess who was already in there? Mom had read an ad in the paper and taken a "spur of the moment" shopping trip to that very store.

This time I could tell *him* what was on his list. I could tell him things he hadn't even told me! He was no longer a skeptic. In fact, he would be a believer for a long time.

And all thanks to a very determined mother! She told me a few months later that he no longer believed his friends; he had evidence to the contrary and argued passionately to make his case. He knew better. He had seen the same Santa everywhere he had been for the past two years, all because his mom didn't want his childhood to end too soon.

Why? Because she loved him.

The One That Almost Didn't Get Away

When I'm out talking about FODA or about Santa, I like to say that I've had 88,000 kids on my lap and they've all gone home with their parents.

Well, the truth is, there was a time when one of them almost went home with me!

There are several families who have been coming to Stone Mountain every year since I've been there. I even have one family that comes all the way from Minnesota every year. It's not easy to keep up with folks when you only see them for a minute or two once a year, but some of them I do recognize.

Some families have a tradition of getting a picture of their kids with Santa every year, no matter how old the kids are. One of those families had come for four years. Their youngest was twelve in 1994, and the oldest was twenty. In 1995 they were back, and this time they had a surprise, a new baby about a month old. The four kids took their positions for the picture, and then Mom handed me the sleeping baby.

I said to her, "Surprise, surprise, huh, Mom?"

"Yeah, you better believe it," she answered ruefully.

When Dad was finished with the pictures, he made a quick exit. Mom ushered the big kids out and followed after them.

I was left holding the baby!

Heidi was the elf that night, and she came over and said, "Got a keeper, huh, Santa?"

"I guess so. Mom just walked out and left him or her," I answered. "I'm sure she'll be back in a minute."

But she wasn't. Five minutes went by as Heidi and I argued over who should be holding the little one. Then we took turns. More time passed.

Some of the people in line were beginning to get a bit edgy. I was about to hand the baby back to Heidi and go on with the folks in line when suddenly the exit door burst open and in came Mom, wheezing and gasping like a sprinter after a race.

"I'm sorry," she gasped while reaching for her little one.

I said, "Aw, heck, Mom, I was sure we had a keeper. Mrs. Claus would be so excited to get a little one like this."

"I'm sorry," she said again, cradling the sound little sleeper in her arms. "I'm embarrassed to tell you this, but we got all the way to the car and it wasn't until I saw the car seat before I remembered we had another one. I can't believe I did that."

She turned and was gone before I stopped laughing enough to answer. But I would always have this one to remember as the one who nearly didn't get away.

Touched by an Angel

I was talking to a boy of six when I first noticed her in the line. She was up next and was so excited she could hardly contain herself. She skipped from one foot to the other and wrung her hands as fast as she could. The smile on her face would have lit up downtown.

The thing that was different about her was that she was about thirty-five years old.

The boy on my lap appeared to be her brother, so when I finished taking his order, I asked, "Is that your sister?"

"Yeah," he answered, "but you don't have to talk to her. She ain't right in the head, never has been."

"Well, I will talk to her," I said. "Santa loves all the kids, no matter how old they are."

The boy immediately jumped off my lap and yelled to a woman standing nearby, "He wants to talk to Rachel!"

His sis started toward me, but the woman pushed between us.

"You don't have to mess with her," the woman yelled. "She's retarded, ain't never been right!"

I reached out and took the yelling woman by the arm. I drew her close. "This is your daughter?" I whispered with a nod.

The woman nodded back.

"Yes," I echoed. "She's also a child of God, who loves her as much as he does any of his children—and so does this Santa. So I am as thrilled to talk to her as I am to talk to any of God's children."

The woman's jaw dropped open. Then I turned to Rachel and gestured for her to approach.

Rachel dropped all of her considerable weight on my left leg, and I struggled to make sure she was safely perched. I asked her the usual questions, and when I asked what she wanted for Christmas, she gave me the same list virtually every five-year-old girl had given that day: "A Barbie doll, a Barbie house, some Barbie clothes, and some surprises."

I listened intently to her words, but it was Rachel's soul that was speaking loudest at that moment. She may have been mentally impaired, but her real handicap was the family into which she had been born.

When she finished her list, I gave her a gentle hug and told her that God loved her and so did Santa Claus. I told her to be a good girl, and she nodded vigorously. Then I said, "Promise?"

The smile on her face lit the room. "I promise!" she announced so fervently, and I knew. Scenes from the original Christmas story crowded my view of the loud mother and busy shoppers around Stone Mountain, of the flashing lights and kids lined up to tell me their Christmas wishes.

I had been entertaining an angel, unawares.

The Child That Stays with You

I don't know how long they had been there before I first noticed them—a young mother pushing her son around and around the set in his wheelchair. Once I noticed them, I saw them make a couple of circuits around the set. The mom would push around to where she could get a good view, then she would stop, watch for a few minutes, and push on.

I tried to get her attention when I didn't have a child on my lap, but the gap between kids was very brief, and I couldn't make eye contact. Then I looked up after bidding a youngster to be a good girl, and our eyes locked. I waved at her to make sure, and she waved back. Then I gestured for her to come around the set and up the exit. She nodded and turned in

the Red Suit Diaries

that direction. I reached out for the next child and gave him my full attention.

When I finished with his order, I released him toward the exit, and there was the mom with her son in the wheelchair. I motioned to the elf working the line to hold up for a moment and gestured for Mom to come up. She pushed the wheelchair to me, and I saw that her son was about four and severely disabled. I asked her if I could take him out of his chair. She looked shocked, then agreed.

I unhooked his support straps and lifted him into my arms, cradling him carefully. His mom knelt at my feet. I looked into his beautiful eyes that were fixed on my face and said, "Who is this, Mom?"

"This is Cody," she answered. "Cody Cooper."

"Tell me about Cody, Mom," I whispered.

She answered matter-of-factly. "Cody is a near-drowning survivor. We had a brief rain shower a couple of years ago, and when it was over, we went outside to work in the yard. Cody wandered off for a few minutes, and we found him face down in a puddle about two inches deep. He's a very special little boy."

I could see the "special" deep in Cody's eyes.

"Cody, you just don't know how special you are to this Santa," I whispered. "I know you have been a very good boy, and we are going to see if we can't find some very special things for you for Christmas."

A smile crept across the boy's face. Mom looked like she was about to burst. I felt like I would too.

I motioned her out of the way and lifted up Cody for a picture. Then I signaled to the photographer that the pictures were free—and that I wanted one for myself. Pretty soon, an elf was signaling me to hurry up, since there was a long line of people waiting. So I gently placed Cody back into his chair, replaced the straps, and leaned over to kiss him on the forehead. His mom managed to say through her tears and her constricted throat, "We'll be back."

I nodded, and they were gone.

A few days later I saw them again, watching from near the exit. I motioned to them, and after a couple more kids, Cody was back in my arms. This time his mom had brought her camera, and she took several quick pictures.

the ℛed Suit Diaries

"Cody couldn't stand it," she said. "He had to see you again and bring you these." She handed me a Ziploc bag full of homemade cookies. Then they were gone again.

A few days later I was engrossed in an interview with a little one. The moment it was finished, there was Cody's mom, handing me an envelope with pictures in it. "Cody wanted you to have these," she said, then stepped back and was gone before I could shout, "Thank you!" I had intended to ask her for the family's phone number and had missed my chance.

Several kids later, I had a brief moment and looked at the pictures, which showed a Cody so joyful he shone. On the back of one photo was their phone number.

I smiled as I dialed the number the next morning. I learned that Cody's mom was Judy and his dad was Henry, and that even though they faced some tough times they were still smiling too. Cody's health care had wiped them out financially, and then Henry had lost his job. But recently he'd found another job, and things were looking up.

I wanted to be sure, though. I offered to make any repairs or adjustments to Cody's wheelchair, and then I offered to pay them a home visit sometime before Christmas.

A couple of weeks later I went by their apartment after church and before my shift at the mall. I brought a small gift and wore a red sport coat, white shirt, and tie. Cody was just as mesmerized by that as he was by my Santa getup. You would have thought the little gift I'd brought was five pounds of gold.

So began a long friendship.

Judy brought Cody by the house after Christmas, and I tuned up his wheelchair and reset his seating a little bit. We had a great visit, and Annie and Cody fell for each other immediately.

Judy was quite stoic when she talked about Cody; she said his injury had been a gift from God and that she had learned more about love and giving since then than in her entire life before that. She said she had no idea how long God was going to leave Cody with her but that she was going to love him as hard as she could for as long as she was permitted.

the ℛed Suit Diaries

Through the years, the Coopers, Santa, and Mrs. Claus stayed in touch. There are still visits among us, exchanges of pictures, and always that Christmas visit to see Cody's own personal Santa.

Cody is in school now, and although his general condition hasn't improved, he's still a happy boy, proud of his big brother role to the little sister that Judy and Henry later adopted.

God has chosen to let Cody stay with his mom and dad longer than they imagined, and it's impossible to tell who is happier about that. Every child, after all, is a gift, and Cody's family is just a little better at knowing that.

Lindsey Brown

At Gwinnett Place Mall the Santa set was located on the lower level, with a large opening in the upper level just above the set. People would gather along the railing up there and watch the proceedings down below. When I got a chance I would look up and wave to the crowd.

One day I spotted two women leaning against the railing. There was a child in a wheelchair between them. I waved, and the women waved back.

Then in a while I looked up again, and they were still there. I waved again and gestured for them to come down. The women looked at each other and spoke but didn't move.

After a few more kids I looked up again, and still they stood glued to the rail. This time I waved and gestured more energetically. They waved back.

I became determined to get that child onto my lap! When I got my next free moment, I raised myself off my throne, dragging my microphone wires with me, pointed to them, and yelled at the top of my considerable voice, "Go down the elevator and up the exit!"

They detached themselves from the railing and headed for the elevator, which was to my left down the exit walkway. I went on with some other kids until I saw the wheelchair close up on my left. The child was a little girl of about four, beautiful with long blonde hair and a smile that nearly split her face in

the Red Suit Diaries

two. It was clear that she was quite impaired with multiple disabilities.

"Who is this, Mom?" I asked, never taking my eyes off her child.

Mom answered, "This is Lindsey Ann Brown, Santa. She is four years old, and she loves Santa Claus."

I reached for the straps securing Lindsey's feet to the footrests and said, "Can I put Lindsey on my lap, Mom?"

"Sure you can, but you don't have to."

"Yes, I do," I responded. "You see, Santa loves Lindsey too." I gently loosened the butterfly brace on her chest and carefully lifted her onto my lap. I cradled her head with one hand and told our photographer to take a full (free) package of pictures for them. Then I laid her fragile little body across my lap and said, "Tell me about Lindsey, Mom."

Mom described all the problems Lindsey had, and I asked what her prognosis was. Mom answered, "We don't really know. The doctors didn't think she would live this long. We've just decided that Lindsey is a gift from God, and we're just going to love her as long as we have her."

Childlike Faith

I found myself saying, through a greatly constricted throat, "Well, somehow I believe that you are going to have Lindsey to love for a long, long time."

Other people were waiting, so I began to put Lindsey back into her chair. I noticed that her positioning pads needed adjusting. I told this to her mom, and she said they hadn't been able to afford to have that done.

I took one of the coloring books we were giving to each child and wrote my name and home phone number on it. I handed it to Lindsey's mom and said, "Call this guy tomorrow, and he'll adjust it for free." They thanked me and left. I gestured to the next kid in line and went on.

The following morning I answered the phone in my wheelchair shop, and a hesitant female voice asked for me, then said, "I don't quite know how to say this, but the Santa at Gwinnett Place Mall told me to call you and said that you could adjust my granddaughter's wheelchair."

"That's true," I said. "You see, I'm the Santa at Gwinnett Place Mall." Then I told her about the ministry Annie and I were doing, made an appointment, and gave her directions to our house.

142

At the appointed time they came and brought me a framed poem that Lindsey's mom, whose name was Jane, had written. Jane told me that they had hesitated to come down from their railing because the previous year, at a different mall, they had waited in line for almost an hour, and when it was their turn, the Santa took one look at Lindsey and said, "No way, I'm not about to touch that kid!" Then he had gestured them out of his way and turned to the next child in line.

I was shocked and appalled, and I resolved then and there that I would never do such a horrid thing. Every child that I saw would be treated like any other child, with as much love as I could muster.

Jane and I talked a couple of times the next year, and when she didn't bring Lindsey to see me at the American Fare store I called her after the season and took a doll to Lindsey at home. Later, I visited Lindsey and her mom and dad in Scottish Rite Children's Medical Center when she had an extremely brutal surgical procedure to straighten her compound curvature of the spine.

We are still in touch with the Browns, and Lindsey is doing quite well, going to school and becoming quite a young lady. She can drive her own electric wheelchair and still hasn't lost that dazzling smile.

At the Grapevine

One of the women I'd met at DHR gave me a call one day and invited me to come to Lake City, South Carolina. Annie and I agreed to go there in October for five days of taking pictures in her gift shop. I had been to Lake City when I was selling and calling on hospitals, but I couldn't remember one thing about it except that it had a nice hospital.

Jean's shop was called "The Grapevine," and Annie and I decided to run a recon trip that evening so we wouldn't be running around lost the next morning. We found the place easily and were charmed immediately.

Jean and a couple of her helpers were there, so we went in to say hello and coordinate any last-minute arrangements. The shop was delightful inside, and Jean made us feel very welcome. We liked the photo

144   the Red Suit Diaries

setup too. A simple white background, a wide wooden bench with an adequate cushion, and a huge toy soldier Jean's husband had made.

The next morning Annie and I donned our Claus outfits and went to the Grapevine earlier than scheduled. We walked in and met our photography team. We didn't know it at that moment, but we were about to make some lifetime friends. Dave Marcum is a dead ringer for Ray Stevens—dark hair and beard, thin, a real bundle of energy. His wife, Fran, immediately charmed us with her smile and personality.

I know a little something about photography (I taught it at Clayton State College in their adult education program for a while). One of the things that is very difficult to teach and even harder to learn is a skill called "touch"—the ability to anticipate action and fire the shutter to catch the event at the best possible moment. At about the third kid on my lap, I realized that the flash was going off at the precise moment it needed to. Clearly this was no ordinary photo team.

Dave was masterful at getting and keeping the kids' attention and working a smile out of even the smallest ones. The interviews went just as well. We were a great team. We found out that first day that Dave and Fran also love the Lord and trust him completely. We have learned to love each other as brothers and sisters in Christ, and we all know that we can share that love forever. What joy!

James Franklin King

I didn't see his mom when she came the first time. She told me later she was driving through Lake City when she saw a sign for the Grapevine and remembered she needed a gift for someone. She didn't know that Santa was there until she walked in. She looked through the door as I was talking to a child and couldn't believe her eyes. She watched for a moment, thinking of her son, James Franklin King.

James Franklin was four years old. His mom had been told that he was slightly retarded, and he had always expressed a fear of many things. One big fear was of Santa Claus. Mom had many pictures of her older sons on Santa's lap, but none of her youngest son. After watching me for a few minutes, she forgot about buying a gift and took off for home, twenty-six miles away, to get James Franklin.

I didn't see her right away when she came back with her son, but I did notice him immediately when he came in the door. He was dressed like Little Lord Fauntleroy, but that wasn't what drew my attention.

His brow was furrowed in a near frown so severe that his eyebrows were almost touching. He had his hands raised up beside his head, and he would cover his ears at the slightest noise.

For some reason this reaction seemed familiar to me. Then I remembered "Fighting for Georgie," an article in *Reader's Digest* about a child with a hearing disorder that caused her to hear some background noises as painfully loud. It depended on the pitch of the sound. Georgie had developed some strategies to protect herself from sudden assaults on her eardrums—she withdrew from people whose voices hurt her, she avoided places with frightening sounds, and she was always ready to cover her ears. Her recovery from this condition was dramatic and complete, when

she got the right treatment. James Franklin seemed to be just like Georgie in the article.

My wife, Annie, is not only the smartest human being I have ever known, but she is also the kindest person on earth. She hadn't read the *Reader's Digest* article, but she knew that James Franklin was a special child. She approached him very slowly and talked to him in a low, soft, evenly modulated voice, intuitively doing the right thing.

He calmed down, and when she suggested that he go with her to talk to Santa, he nodded his assent. That's when I noticed his mom. She had raised both hands to her mouth and was moments away from bursting into sobs.

Annie led him by the hand to within my reach, but I did not raise my hands from my lap. Annie said, "Santa, this is James Franklin King. Isn't he a big boy this year?"

I used the same monotone voice Annie was using. "Yes, he sure is. He grew up a lot since last Christmas, didn't he?" I still didn't touch him. He had his hands ready by his ears.

"Have you been a good boy, James Franklin?" I asked.

He nodded.

"Would you like to sit on my lap?"

He nodded again. I touched him lightly on the shoulder. There was a momentary flinch, and then I could feel him begin to relax. I touched him more firmly then moved him closer and let him lean back against my leg. I signaled Fran to wait a moment for the picture. I wanted him on my lap.

We began to talk, and in a moment his hands went down and he was more relaxed. I lowered my leg, slid him up on it, then raised it back up again.

Fran and Dave were ready, and James Franklin didn't even notice the flash. He was talking to Santa! (And his mama was about ready to lose it.)

He said to me, "No ho-hos. No ho-hos, please!" I knew why he had been afraid of Santa in the past. Santa was probably overdoing the ho-hoing! That sound could have been one that was painful for him. He wasn't afraid of the man, he was afraid of the ho-hos!

Childlike Faith

149

Fifteen minutes passed before any other kids came in. I told James Franklin that he was my very special buddy and that I loved him. Then Annie took his hand and led him away.

His mom came to me and hugged my neck. Her tears wet my ears. I asked her to tell me about James Franklin, and that's when she told me he had been diagnosed as retarded.

"That boy has a hearing disorder," I said. Before I could say anything else, she dropped to her knees at my feet and gasped for breath. I continued. "There's a condition some kids have that makes them very sensitive to certain frequencies of sound. I believe he has it."

Mom grabbed my hand. She told me that a nearby medical center was going to have a hearing screening program in early November, and she had already signed James Franklin up for testing. If he had the problem, they would be doing the hearing retraining in January.

I said to her, "I'll tell you now that James Franklin will be in that training, and you'll not believe what a difference it's going to make in your son."

More tears and another hug. Then she asked me for our address so she could let us know how it went. I gave her a FODA business card, and she gathered her little boy, giving Annie a hug on her way out.

In the middle of November we got a letter. Indeed, James Franklin had been diagnosed with the hearing disorder, and he was at the top of the list for the retraining. Mom could hardly wait for January.

Right after Christmas we got another letter. This one had a copy of a front-page article from a newspaper. I was shocked by the article. James Franklin's mom had told a reporter that this Santa had told her things he could only have known if he was an angel. She ascribed several other powers to me, none of which were based on reality. It was obvious that the poor woman was delusional!

But then Annie convinced me that God had used me to help someone. It had been no coincidence that I had read the *Reader's Digest* article, and certainly nothing in my power brought it to mind at the very moment I needed to recall it. All those "happenstances" that had brought James Franklin to my knee—were they part of a plan? Were Annie and I being used to bring comfort to a worried mother and a beautiful little boy right when they needed it most, right in this glorious season of such promise to the world? Were we being used to make the message of this season's hope more real for James Franklin and the whole King family? Time would tell.

And it did. The next summer James Franklin's mom called and invited Annie and me to use a family cabin at Murrells Inlet south of Myrtle Beach. She told us she would have a surprise for us when we got there. We thought the cabin was a nice enough surprise.

Right after we arrived at the cabin, Mom came by and had my little buddy with her. We had a warm reunion. His hands were not grabbing at his ears. He seemed much more mature, more confident and proud of himself. Eagerly Mom handed him a book. "Show Santa your surprise, darling," she said quietly.

Quickly, confidently, James Franklin opened the book and began to read. He labored along like any five-year-old would do. But he was reading just like any other five-year-old boy. He wasn't reading like he was retarded. He was reading just like a regular kid.

And Annie and I were like how any other regular adults would have been at that moment. We were blubbering our eyes out.

Restaurant Tours

Jean Lee and her husband, Ken, were wonderful hosts. They had contacted several restaurants in the area and promised them a visit from Santa Claus if they would be willing to provide free meals for Santa and Mrs. Claus. They all agreed. We made our first stop at the Red Barn, a family-owned steak house, and we had a ball. This was farming country, where the folks are the salt of the earth.

We developed a fun routine for our visits to restaurants. We let our hosts go in first and get seated so they could enjoy the show. After a few minutes Annie and I would enter and begin to make our way around the room to speak to everyone there. We visited the kids, of course, and had a great amount of fun with the grown-ups too, handing out suckers to everyone.

Most adults considered themselves much too sophisticated to be interested in Santa, but we took them on dead center. We accused them of not being good little girls and boys. If there was a crowd at a table, I'd pick out one and tell the rest of them that I remembered that one when he was a little boy or girl and that he was a real rounder.

When we sat down to eat at the Red Barn, we were all treated to a fabulous meal. During that time several kids came up to talk to Santa, and we invited them all to come to the Grapevine the next day. After the meal I made my way into the kitchen to visit with the cooks and dishwashers. After some laughter and suckers all around, we made our way out the door and to the Days Inn for a much-needed night of sleep.

The next day we went to Prosser's Cafeteria for lunch. It was another wonderful visit. The fried chicken at Prosser's is impossible to beat—absolutely delicious.

That evening we went to Country Cousins Barbecue. Woo-ooo-eee, was that ever good. Sitting nearby there was a giant of a man in bib overalls. His wife looked me in the eye as I approached their table and ever so slightly shook her head. I went on up to the table and said hello. She looked. He kept eating. I said I had come by to check up on them and left two suckers on the table, admonishing them to be good kids. He never stopped eating.

Later, while we were eating, they got up to leave. I watched as he picked up the suckers, handed one to her, and headed for the door. As he went by our table, a deep, rumbling voice said something that sounded very much like, "Merry Christmas, Santa." He never looked our way or slowed down. But somewhere, deep down inside that gruff exterior, beat the heart of a little boy. Just don't tell him I said that!

We would go back to all of these places again and again over the years. The food and the fun are always wonderful, but the fellowship with the customers and the folks who own the places is always so very special. We've talked about how heaven has got to be like this—a welcoming, warm, loving fellowship with the joy of celebrating together the birth of our Savior. There won't be a Santa Claus, but Jesus will be there, and that will be what makes it so incredibly special.

Santa Rides Again

Everyone knows Santa gets around using reindeer, right? Well, in some European countries, Santa gets around on a horse.

Back in my youth I was quite an equestrian—not in the Olympic sense, in the ranch hand sense. Some of my friends and I used to spend Friday afternoons rounding up the horses and cows on a big farm near my house. We separated the horses into corrals and got them ready for their owners to come out on Saturday and Sunday to ride.

I had last sat on a horse in 1981 when I attended a national sales meeting of my company. As far as I was concerned I never intended to ride again. Then Dave and Fran had a wild idea. They had a horse, and they thought Santa and Mrs. Claus on and around their horse would make for some great pictures.

Although I was quite confident aboard any horse, Annie had no equine experience and was wary of any animal that was bigger than she was (including me!). She was less than enthusiastic about the idea of the pictures, at least ones with her in it. But being the trouper that she is, she was willing to at least give it a try, just as long as she didn't have to sit astride the beast.

Dave didn't help matters when he told us the horse was a broodmare and had a young colt. She was also a bit on the skittish side, and he had some question as to how she would react when the flash went off. Oh boy, I could just see the thing tossing me off her back and trampling Annie. But that's showbiz. Let's try it!

Dave and I rode in our van out to the barn to get the mare saddled up and ready. It took a while to separate the colt from his mom and get the bridle and saddle on. I found out that I hadn't forgotten how to do a proper cinch knot, and we got the horse properly prepared.

I spent some time right at her head, letting her check me out and letting her know I wasn't afraid of her. She didn't like the bit in her mouth and was working up quite a froth, so I had to be careful not to get any of her slobber on my outfit.

I'd like to tell you I did a quick swinging mount into the saddle. But that would be stretching it. I couldn't get my foot into the stirrup and my hand on the pommel at the same time. Seems there was too much of my "little round belly that shakes when I laugh like a bowl full of jelly" in the way! Finally Dave intervened and gave me a boost, and I was aboard.

The mare didn't much like all this weight on her and was trying to decide whether to buck or run when I let her know that I knew what that bit in her mouth was for. She got the message that I was in control and knew what to do. She calmed right down and behaved like a lady . . . for the moment.

Annie and Fran came riding out in Fran's van, and as Annie got out I could see the apprehension on her face. Dave escorted Annie closer to the horse and helped the two of them get acquainted. Annie managed to rub the mare's nose and say, "Wow, it's so soft." Helpful Santa shouted, "Watch out for the slobber!" Well, I was trying to help. Annie only had two Mrs. Claus outfits with her, while I had three. But my shout startled the mare, and she pitched her head and shoved Annie, nearly knocking her over and forcing her to step backward about four steps. I was afraid Annie wouldn't get near her again.

the Red Suit Diaries

I tightened the reins, spun the mare around, and told her to settle down and behave. I turned her broadside toward Fran for the first shot, and Annie crept up to her and grabbed her bridle. Turning quickly toward Fran she said, "Cheese." Fran took the shot.

To our profound relief the mare did not react at all to the flash. Fran shot as fast as she could get us lined up and still. Annie held on to the bridle firmly, and the mare didn't fight her anymore. I knew that Fran's fantastic "touch" with her camera was getting some great shots. Soon she said, "Got it!"

Annie stepped away daintily but quickly toward Fran's van.

Then I had this vision of Santa riding at a full gallop across the pasture, his hat streaming behind him and the mare's mane and tail streaming out behind her. I could see myself calling out, "Hi ho, reindeer, away!" What a picture that would make. I knew that all I had to do was release the reins, dig my heels into the side of the mare, and shout, "Hi-yaah!" and we'd be off. I shouted to Fran, "Watch this!"

With that, the momentary urge passed, and I turned and dropped out of the saddle before I got carried away and did something stupid.

So much for "riding the range once more, toting my old .44." In the song, a .44 is a "shootin' arn." In real life, that's my waist size! Ahhh, reality.

Santa's Surprise

Everybody knows that Santa only comes around at Christmas. But not everyone knows that he sometimes shows up for birthday parties too. I already told you about one birthday appearance for a little guy. This story is about a birthday appearance for a grown-up girl.

During our Lake City visit in October 1994, Annie and I staged a little birthday surprise party for Dave in our motel room. Fran told us then that she had never had a birthday party in her life. How sad, we both thought. Later during that visit we learned that Fran's birthday was January 8. We decided we were going to give her the party of a lifetime.

That year we had a delightful teenage girl named Sheila Bailey helping on the Santa set, and we had met her parents, Elaine and "Beetle" Bailey, and gotten their address and phone number. On the way home we discussed our strategy. It was imperative that neither Fran nor Dave found out about our plan, and we were confident we could count on the Bailey clan to help pull it off.

It was two weeks before Christmas when I called the Baileys. Elaine got all excited and said she would arrange for a place and contact as many people as she could think of who knew Fran. We told her we would bring all the party hats and favors and a cake.

I called her back a week later, and she said the party would be at Country Cousin's Barbecue and that about forty people could be expected. We were ecstatic. Elaine was the right person for that job for sure—with everything she had to do to prepare her household for Christmas, she still had found time to make someone else happy.

I called again a week later, and she was even more excited. It looked like there could be fifty people, and someone had offered to bake a birthday cake. Boy,

was that something! Annie and I wanted to throw a party, and someone else was doing all the work.

We called again on the seventh, and Elaine said everything was well under control. The party was scheduled for 8:00. The guests, including us, were to arrive at 7:30 to decorate and be there ahead of the guests of honor.

Fran and Dave had been asked to take pictures at a "high school reunion" being held at Country Cousins and were told to be there at 8:00. The crowd could be as high as sixty!

Annie and I left home the next morning, a Monday, and drove to Lake City. When we got to Country Cousins, we set up the table with party plates and napkins, party hats and noise makers and streamers all around the place. I visited with the staff and the patrons, passing out suckers and dispensing Santa lore all around while I nervously awaited the arrival of our guests of honor.

Only one thing could dampen the excitement at this point. You guessed it. Rain! And it did. Boy, did it! There was a sudden downpour right at 8:00, but just as suddenly, it was over.

Several people were watching through the blinds, and I couldn't resist, so I went over and peeped out myself. I felt like I was willing them to arrive. They didn't. For another twenty minutes.

I was in near cardiac arrest when they finally pulled up to the door. As they started to unload the photo equipment, someone in the parking lot said to them, "You better get inside before it starts to rain again."

Dave came in first and saw me immediately. He had a "what is going on here?" look on his face. Then Fran came in. Right on cue, everyone yelled "Surprise!" and then launched into "Happy Birthday," led by a very off-key Santa.

Fran jumped when everyone yelled, and she scanned the room quickly as the singing started and saw me. She started to cry and kept it up for the better part of the next two hours. Me too.

There were hugs and more hugs all around as she and Dave made their way to their seats. We sang again, and everyone went through the chow line. There were testimonials and short and long speeches and party hats and noise makers and wonderful barbecue and even better fellowship.

There were presents and candles and a cake and everything that a birthday party ought to have. Fran was a little girl again, and all the birthdays with no parties were forgotten in the glory of this one. Annie and I were just grateful that we were able to be part of this wonderful time for Fran—this plugging up of the holes that had been in her life for a long, long time.

This was another glimpse of heaven.

Santa at the Steak House

People sometimes ask if it bothers me to be out in public and have kids or adults make some comment about Santa. The truth is that if it bothered me, I could just shave and it would never happen again. But I won't ever do that! As long as I am physically able, I will keep enjoying every precious moment. Like this one.

Annie and I were heading home after a busy week in Lake City. As soon as the last picture was taken, we changed clothes (I put on blue jeans and a green shirt, Annie put on blue pants and a non–Christmas

the Red Suit Diaries

sweater), gave our friends Dave and Fran a proper good-bye, and hit the road. We didn't get very far (we never do) before we got hungry, so we decided to stop at a family steak house.

Several people did double takes as we entered and went through the line. But no one said anything. When we got to the cashier, she looked up, gasped, and said, "My goodness, you look like . . ."

I quickly raised my forefinger to my lips and said, "Shhh, don't tell anyone I'm here, OK?" She nodded, mouth still agape.

"Promise?" I said. She nodded again, and I handed her a sucker, saying, "Don't forget, don't tell anybody, OK?"

She nodded, holding the sucker out in front of her, mouth still open. Fortunately, she had rung up our trays before she had looked up. I had the exact change, which I handed her, and we picked up our trays and headed for a table.

We went by a large family group, and I heard a child say, "There's Santa Claus." I shushed him and looked at the rest of the family, saying, "Shhh, don't tell anybody."

When we got seated I looked around, and every eye in the place was fastened on us. I waved briefly and did another, "Shhh."

When we went to the salad bar, I smiled at folks along the way and waved at a few kids. Then we said our blessing as we always do and started to eat. I could feel the eyes staring, but I didn't look up.

A family went past and selected a table behind us. The son was about eleven and the daughter about seven. He looked at us with a smug "I'm not impressed" look. The daughter hadn't spotted us until she was right beside us, and she stopped in her tracks three feet away, stared for a moment, then realized what she was doing and hurried to join her family.

Annie could watch them from her seat, and she described a very animated exchange among all of them with the girl nodding, the boy shaking his head, and the parents shrugging their shoulders.

They all went to the salad bar, and on the way back the daughter almost ran into a table with her plate because she was staring at me. In a few minutes the dad went to the salad bar alone. Annie went to the salad bar too, stood across from him, and asked him

the Red Suit Diaries

the names of his kids. He told her Kevin and Danielle. She told him we were going to have some fun with them if it was OK, and he quickly agreed. She waited until he had returned to his seat, then came back to our table with this information.

We soon finished our meal and started to leave. I turned and went over to the family's table. "Danielle," I said, "I've noticed that you've been a very good girl, and I want you to have this sucker."

Danielle smiled, looked at her brother, and said, "I told you so!"

There was a smirk all over the boy's face. He shook his head.

"Kevin, you must learn not to be so skeptical," I said.

At the sound of his name, Kevin very nearly dropped his teeth! His mouth flew open, and he sucked in air audibly.

Continuing, I said, "You just never know who may be watching. That's why you always have to be a good boy. Here's a sucker for trying. Keep it up."

Kevin still hadn't started to breathe, and he couldn't even reach for the sucker. I laid it on the table.

"See you soon," I said and headed for the door.

As we walked to the exit, every eye in the place was fixed on us. I stopped, made a big wave, and said, "Merry Christmas to all and to all a good night!" We went out the door to a resounding ovation.

Now, go back and read that again and tell me one place where I claimed to be anybody but myself. Did I say I was Santa Claus? Did I wear anything to bring attention to myself other than have a beard?

But wasn't it fun?

See why I'll never shave again?

What Santa Can Give

One of the toughest things any Santa is ever called to do is visit kids in the hospital. It is at the same time tremendously rewarding and agonizingly painful.

My first visit was to Scottish Rite Children's Hospital in Atlanta. I was met at the door by two children's wagons full of teddy bears donated by a local bank. I was to visit every child and give them a teddy bear. Easy, huh? Sure.

A public relations staff member accompanied me on these rounds, and as we made our way from room to room, I could feel her becoming more and more of a nurturing person than a public relations person. I could certainly feel myself becoming more and more filled with a feeling of frustration that I couldn't do more than hand out stupid teddy bears!

About halfway through our tour, I walked into the room of a teenage boy. The nurse told me he had been back from surgery for a couple of hours so it was OK to go on in. I pushed open the door and heard the unmistakable sound of violent vomiting. Immediately I saw that his mother was holding him by the back of the head, and he was heaving into a kidney-shaped bowl that had just filled up to the brim.

I looked around the room and saw another bowl on the sink, just out of the mother's reach. I dropped the inadequate teddy bear on the bed and lunged for the empty bowl, then handed it to her, taking the full one from her trembling hand.

"Here you go, Mom," I said softly.

I dumped the full one into the commode and washed it out in the sink, then swapped with her again. Then again. Then again. Finally, the vomiting stopped, and I said, "I just came by to let both of you know that Mrs. Claus and I are praying for you."

This time Mom did the lunging and threw her arms around my neck. Through her sobs I heard her say, "Thank you so much! I always knew that you were real."

A Scripture from Isaiah came to mind: "I came to comfort the hurting." Wasn't that what Jesus said he wanted us to do? I said a silent prayer, "Thank you Lord, for this opportunity to demonstrate your love."

I continued from room to room, knowing that I wasn't there just to give out teddy bears. I told all the rest of the kids and the parents that Santa loved them and more importantly God loved them and that I was praying for them. I hugged kids, moms, and dads. I spoke Spanish to some parents from Honduras who were there with their child who was having some serious birth defects corrected for free by loving doctors. I held a tiny girl dying of AIDS. I touched two siblings in comas from an auto accident (caused by a drunk driver) that had killed their mom.

the ℞ed Suit Diaries

I couldn't heal these kids like Jesus had healed so many people, but I could demonstrate his love—the love he had shown to me could be passed around. And no matter how many kids were in this hospital, I had been given an endless supply of love to pass on to them.

I went out the doors of that hospital as Jolly Old Saint Nick, but in my car I cried all the way home.

A Lesson in Love

Inspired by that one hospital visit, I was ready to go on others. The next time I took along my red bag filled with stuffed animals that had been donated to our ministry.

My friend Dave went along with me, and we made our way to the children's floor. The onlookers couldn't believe what they were seeing. It seems that naturally bearded Santas are a real rarity in that neck of the woods. The staff inside the hospital had the same reaction, and when we got to the children's floor a near riot broke out among the nurses over who would accompany me as I visited the kids.

We made the rounds without incident. As I visited each child, I reached into my bag and pulled out whatever toy touched my hand. In every case it was perfect for that particular child. I did all I could to spread some love around to all the kids and the staff too. That part was easy.

Then I met a tiny child about two years old. She had some minor facial birth defects and was playing contentedly on a blanket spread on the floor under her bed. The nurses told me her mother had checked into the hospital under an assumed name, then walked out shortly after her baby was born and had never come back. The child literally had been in the hospital all her life.

She had been named and nurtured by the staff, who cared for her and took turns playing with her and rocking her in a rocking chair. She was a happy, typical two-year-old. They had tried to find a foster home or an adoptive family, but they gave up after a while. I asked who was paying for her care, and they told me they had stopped keeping records. They just took care of her.

I realized there was no chance of me teaching these people about love. They already knew all about it.

Questions and Answers

Kids ask me a million questions. Most of them, fortunately, are about Santa, Mrs. Claus, the elves, the reindeer, the toy shops, and other things about Santa's life. As long as I am creative and consistent, those are the easy questions. The hard ones are those about the kids themselves—things they think Santa ought to know.

One day Annie and I were having dinner in a restaurant with good friends from our church. We were having an animated, post-dinner conversation, and I was leaning forward, elbows on the table, when I felt a gentle tapping on my right leg.

I knew immediately that it wasn't Annie, since she was seated to my left. I was pretty sure it wasn't my friend Ernie, sitting on my right, because if he wanted to get my attention he would slap me upside the head (besides, I could see both his hands). So I turned and just there folding her arms was a tiny angel.

She had brown hair and brown eyes that seemed to look into my soul. I figured she was about three years old, although she was a bit small for that age.

There was just something about her that seemed more mature than her size.

"Well, hi, sweetie," I said, leaning toward her. "How are you doing?"

She completely ignored my question and had one of her own. "Where are your reindeer?" she demanded in an authoritative voice.

I began my standard answer to that question (I know it's a surprise, but I have heard that one before) while looking around the room to see where this little doll came from. One of my rules is that I never touch a child unless a parent is there to observe. I couldn't see anyone who looked like they belonged to her, so I leaned toward her but didn't touch her.

"Well, sweetie, the reindeer are at the North Pole. It's much too hot for reindeer here in Georgia in August." She gave her head one brisk nod. "OK?" I asked. She did another full nod, dropped her arms from their akimbo position, whirled around 180 degrees, and trotted off toward the corner of the room. Then I saw her dad standing in the shadows. He had been there all the time, watching protectively. I motioned for him to come over, but he was

174

the ℛed Suit Diaries

so intently watching his pride and joy that he missed my gesture. She ran into his arms, and he slid back into his seat, beaming to his wife.

A tougher question, another place. I had listened to a little guy about six as he recited a memorized list. It had six items on it, nothing unique or particularly memorable. I nodded and repeated each item in turn as he reeled them off.

Then I asked if that was all. He said yes, and I eased him off my lap. He took one step, turned back around, and, shaking a finger at me, said, "OK, if you're the real Santa, tell me what my order was."

Horror of horrors, a nightmare had come true. In the line I saw that three of his friends were intently awaiting the results of this challenge.

One of my tricks when I was in grade school and was required to memorize something (and had forgotten to study it) was to ask the teacher if I could be last. I would then listen to all the other kids blunder through their recital of the assignment and repeat it to myself as they went. By the time the last one before me had finished, I had it down cold. Then I would get up and with great emphasis and theatrics do a flawless presentation. That's why the teacher always agreed to let me be last, so I could show the others how to do it right! If she had ever called on me first, I would've been dead meat.

Now I was being asked to recite something I hadn't been trying to memorize. Would it work? I called him by the correct name and then said, "So, you're trying to trap me, is that it?" (I was buying some time to think.) "It's not nice to try to play games with Santa Claus, you know that, don't you?" He nodded. (More time.) He was standing about five feet away from me, so I motioned him to come closer, then reached out and slowly guided him closer until he was standing between my knees. (More time.) Leaning forward I softly recited his list back to him verbatim in the same order he had given it to me. I was almost as surprised as he was. *Thank you, Lord,* I said silently.

He leaped into the air, throwing his hands toward the ceiling. Turning to his cronies he screamed at the top of his voice, "He did it! He did it! He did it! It's him. It's really him!"

But it was in High Point where I faced one of my biggest questions. There was never a big crowd in

the **R**ed Suit Diaries

the store, so I could take my time with kids. I loved that, but sometimes I could've used a little more "line pressure."

On this particular day the crowd had been sparse for a few minutes, so Annie was sitting beside me on the throne chair. (I had built it myself to accommodate both of us.) We were chatting, planning our evening, when into the store came three boys with their mother. The youngest was about eight and the others were twelve and fourteen. I figured they just wanted a quick picture, probably wouldn't want to sit on my lap but would gather around the throne. I motioned to Annie to keep her seat beside me.

As they were walking toward us, the youngest suddenly halted, spread out his arms to stop the others, and issued his challenge. "All right, I want you to tell me my name. If you're really Santa, you'll know my name. So what is it? Tell me my name."

Now, this is not the first time I've heard this question. In all the other cases I've been able to divert their attention and not answer the question at all, or I've been able to find out the answer from a parent or someone else. With smaller kids it's really easy.

I put a shocked look on my face and say, "Oh my goodness, you forgot your name?"

Most immediately say, "No, I didn't either!"

"Oh, yeah? Then tell me what it is."

They usually come back with their name, Rachel, Jack, Amy, or whatever.

Then I look knowingly at them and say, "You're right! You didn't forget after all, did you?"

But somehow, this time I felt like I was flirting with disaster. I decided I would start out by trying to divert his attention. "You don't really think that Santa can keep up with all the kids in spite of how fast they grow, do you? Kids change a lot in a year. I'll bet you can't even keep up with your friends if you only see them once or twice a year."

He shook his head and responded, "It won't work. Tell me my name!"

I thought I would try humor. "Come on, Kara, tell me what you want for Christmas. Some other kids will be here soon. We don't have all day for games, Elizabeth."

He was still shaking his head. "Won't work, tell me my name!" He was becoming more emphatic.

And I was becoming more panicky. I looked at his mom and his brothers. No clues. I looked at my helpers; sometimes they knew these kids. But they were both busily absorbed with customers. No hints there either.

I was looking directly at him when I heard Annie say, "Come on, Danny, the game is over. There are some other kids coming in."

The boy's jaw dropped and his eyes popped open. His defiant posture and attitude evaporated in the instant it took for him to hear his name!

It was all I could do to restrain myself from having the same reaction. How on earth did Annie know or find out his name? I couldn't believe it!

But I was quick enough to know that I'd have to get the answer to that later on. I picked up on his name and said, "Are you ready now, Danny, to tell me what you want for Christmas?"

He nodded yes and came on over, a stunned expression on his face. He looked like a soldier in a losing battle. He sat on my lap and told me his list. When he got off my lap, he took one step, turned, and earnestly beseeched me, "How did you do that?"

I suppressed an answer like, "Heck if I know, ask her" or "I can't believe it myself!" Instead I knowingly tapped my forehead and said, "Knows everything!"

Danny walked away, shaking his head so hard that his whole body was shaking.

Unfortunately, some other kids were in line, and it was over an hour before I could ask Annie how in the world she pulled that one off.

"It was easy," she said. "I got up off the throne, walked around behind the screen, went up to Mom, and asked her what his name was."

I couldn't believe it! "Wait a minute," I said. "You got up and asked his mom?"

"Sure did."

"Well, how did you do that without me or Danny noticing?"

"Easy," my brilliant sweetie said. "You and Danny were so focused on each other I didn't think either of you would notice. And," she said, kissing me on the lips, "I was obviously right. I believe you call that diverting attention, don't you?"

There was Annie's sly grin again. It has a lot of meanings. This time it meant I had been beaten at

the Red Suit Diaries

my own game. I kissed her back right under her beautiful nose!

Yes, I Did!

Annie's all-time favorite movie is *Miracle on 34th Street*. While it's not my all-time favorite, it is high on my list. After all, there are very few people who have not accepted that the Santa at Macy's is an authentic American hero.

I wanted with all my heart to be the Santa at the Macy's store on Peachtree Street in downtown Atlanta. I figured that was as close to New York as I ever wanted to be. And in 1993 I got my chance—I was offered a stint at Macy's while still fulfilling my requirements at Stone Mountain Park.

Macy's had a very nice Santa set with a beautiful, ornately carved throne chair. It made the two I had made for myself look primitive. The only problem was that the seat was solid 3/4-inch plywood with a 2-inch foam cushion. I knew I could never make it through a season on that thing. I took it home the first night and cut out the middle of the plywood base, filled the hole with a woven base, replaced the two-inch foam with four-inch foam, then put the fabric cover back on and tacked it down. The store never noticed the difference, but my tender tush sure did!

Being the Santa at Macy's was indeed different from anywhere else I had worn the red suit. There was a constant parade of downtown office workers through the store, and there were several whom I began to recognize from day to day.

One of the best things about Macy's was that the crowd was never so intense that I couldn't take all the time I needed for each kid. If they were afraid, I could let them work their way to me by having their parents find things for them to show me. There were very few kids who got away if their parents were willing to take the time and let me orchestrate a slow, getting-used-to-Santa routine.

It was also a lot of fun carrying on with the adults. One afternoon three very distinguished, serious-looking gentlemen came into the Christmas shop where we were located. Since I didn't have a kid on my lap I waved cordially at them and said hello.

the R ed Suit Diaries

One of them stopped suddenly and said, "Well, it is you! I want to talk to you about that bicycle I asked for and didn't get in 1927."

I looked thoughtful and stroked my beard a couple of times, saying, "1927, 1927 . . ." Then I pointed at him and exclaimed, "Oh yeah, I remember. So it was you! I got back with an extra bike that year and couldn't remember where it should go. I still have it. Would you like for me to deliver it to you this year?"

He grinned broadly and said, "No, let some little boy have it who'll get some real fun out of it."

"OK, I will surely find one for it. Thanks for letting me off the hook."

He and his friends went on their way, laughing and chatting, slapping each other on the back like they were kids again.

Alas, that would be my only full season at Macy's. Some short-sighted muckety-muck in New York decided there was no reason to have a Santa at the store in Atlanta full-time anymore. There would be more special events, but this was the last season of

Macy's Santa in Atlanta. The end of an era, and it had to be me who finished it off! Oooh, that hurt!

But there were some great encounters while it lasted, and I learned miracles don't have to happen just at Macy's, on the silver screen, or on 34th Street. They could happen wherever I chose to keep my Santa attitude.

One Special Little Lady

When I saw her in line at Macy's, waiting to see Santa, I didn't know that my family was about to get three people bigger. She was a tiny little thing, about two years old, and didn't look very different from thousands of kids I'd had on my lap before.

Most kids her age chickened out when they got within arms' reach of me, but not this one! When it was her turn, she marched right up to me, unfolded her arms, and reached up to let me pick her up and set her on my lap. The instant she was settled she began to chatter.

I didn't have to ask her a question—she just took off. She told me her name was Laura Withers, and she talked about her mommy, who was busily shooting pictures, and her daddy, who worked for President Jimmy Carter. She asked me if I wanted to hear what she wanted for Christmas, and I finally got a word in edgewise by saying yes. She launched into her list, which included some very mature things (for her age).

I could tell by the flashes of the camera that her mom was getting some great pictures. I knew I just had to have some of them; Laura was so animated in her conversation that the pictures were bound to be wonderful.

Then Laura said, "OK, Santa, that's all I have to say, so I will see you later, OK?"

"OK, Laura," I said as I began lowering her to the floor. "You be a good girl now, you hear?"

"Don't you worry, I will," she said, walking primly toward the exit.

Her mom stepped up to me and asked what she had said. When I told her, she cracked up. I asked if I could have some of the pictures, which I now noticed she had taken with a professional model camera. I gave her one of our FODA cards, and she promised to send me a set of her results.

A couple of weeks after Christmas, I got some pictures of Laura in the mail. I sent Mom, whose name I now knew was Vicki, a thank-you note and invited her to bring Laura out to see my office, which has a decided Santa flavor.

A few months went by, and Vicki called to ask if I would attend Laura's third birthday party. I readily agreed. And over the next year, Vicki brought Laura to FODA for a couple of delightful visits. Then she told me that she and Laura were going with her husband to Africa for the Carter Center in an effort to eradicate the ravaging effects of the guinea worm, a parasitic worm that disables thousands of people in central African countries. I was very concerned when they came by to tell me good-bye in the fall of 1993.

Vicki wrote me a long letter during the winter, then walked into my office in midsummer of 1995. It was a great surprise, and Laura was just as charming as a four-year-old. She told me all about how her daddy had "eradicated the guinea worm all by himself and saved thousands of people's lives." There was no doubt who the hero of this little lady was. And rightly so! It was a wonderful effort her dad was making for all mankind.

Vicki told me they were going back to Africa in a month, and that they had come by one more time to say good-bye. Boy, do I hate good-byes!

Another year, another long letter filled with adventures of civil war, customs difficulties, and how a delightful young lady took it all in stride. Then in the summer of 1996 Vicki called me and asked if they could come for a visit. She had two surprises, she said. I figured that it was two African tribal baskets similar to the beautiful one she had brought us the previous summer.

When they arrived at the appointed time, they were announced by Laura dashing in my door and running into my arms, already talking about all her adventures. When Vicki came in the door, one of the surprises revealed itself. She was with child, due very soon as a matter of fact. That was a great surprise.

But I was concerned about how Laura felt about this new person crowding in on her territory. When I asked her what she thought about the baby, she said, "Well, I haven't decided yet. I'm still giving it some thought." This kid was now five years old, but she was talking like she was thirty!

She didn't have very long to think it over. Two weeks after this visit, Vicki called to tell me that the baby, a girl, had arrived safely and that Laura was very excited.

The best news to me was Vicki's second surprise. Her husband's tour of duty in Africa was complete, and they were back home to stay.

Of all the thousands of kids who have been on my lap, none, besides the children in my own family, have been as much a part of my life as this little world traveler, Miss Laura Withers. I'm looking forward to watching her grow up. And now I can look forward to little Megan becoming a young lady as well.

The Mean Mama

As I've already revealed, being Santa is not always easy. The hardest part isn't dealing with the kids. It's trying to handle the parents who are difficult. And some of them are impossible.

the Red Suit Diaries

First, let me assure you that the vast majority of parents are wonderful. They are kind and considerate of me, their kids, and the other people in line around them. But once in a while, I encounter a parent that I'd like to take across my lap and give some old-fashioned discipline. At least, that's what I thought I'd like to do until I met the meanest mama of them all.

The line at Macy's was unusually long that day because a kindergarten class had come to visit Santa. They had brought twenty kids this day in two vans. The kids were well-behaved, as children almost always are when their parents aren't with them. There were individual and then group pictures, so it took a while for them to work through the line.

At first I'd thought the lady in the pink outfit was with the school group. The girl with her was about eight, too old for kindergarten. So I figured one of the other kids must be a sibling, and she was along for the outing.

As I worked my way through the schoolkids, I noticed there had been a disagreement between the mother in pink and her daughter. As time wore on, their words and motions became more strident and animated.

Finally it was their turn. The little girl came right to me, no problem, but she didn't look happy about it. She sat on my lap, and her mother got out her camera. Mom looked through the viewfinder at us and said, "Smile now, Karen." Then she took the camera away from her face and growled, "I said smile, Karen!"

I turned and looked into Karen's face, and it was clear that she was about to erupt in tears.

"Karen, I said look at me and smile!" Mom yelled. Suddenly she lunged toward us and backhanded the child across the face, snatching her off my lap.

"Whoa!" I yelled and tried to grab the child to keep her from falling. I missed, and she sprawled at my feet. Her mother leaned over her and hit her on the back of the head with her open hand. Then she grabbed Karen's arm and dragged her across the floor away from the Santa set and into the Christmas shop sales area. Naturally Karen began to scream at the top of her lungs. I didn't blame her. She had every reason to be screaming. I wanted to scream myself, but I didn't know what I could scream and to whom.

The real question was what I should do. Macy's had a security force, but they were most concerned about shoplifting. I didn't know whether they could handle this one or not. Then I noticed that some longtime Macy's clerks were watching the scene, so I thought maybe they would know what to do. I also thought that surely the woman would beat a hasty exit out of the store.

But the woman didn't leave! She whapped Karen several more times and dragged her up and down the rows of counters. She kept saying, "Yes, you will!"

And Karen kept saying, "No, I won't! You can't make me! Leave me alone! Turn me loose!"

This was elevating into a very ugly situation. People from other parts of the store were coming to see what on earth was happening. I was becoming very uncomfortable—it was hard to be Jolly Old Saint Nick with all this ruckus going on.

Some of the parents and other adults came and made comments to me about it. No one said, "Do something." However, I was getting that message. But what to do? One of the young floor managers came by, and I motioned to him in the direction of the fracas. He only waved and disappeared into the storeroom in the back. Thanks a lot, boss man!

After about twenty agonizing minutes, the woman finally gave up on whatever it was she was trying to do and dragged Karen off across the floor to the escalator. I could still hear them yelling until they got to the ground floor, two levels away.

I never intervened. I did nothing. Nothing at all. Even now, years later, I'm still trying to make up my mind about what I could've done.

Any suggestions?

Believing

Dear Santa,
How many ELves do
you have? I belive in
you! You are the
nicest man # in
the world.

Love Cassandra

P.S.
U R 2 nice 2 B4
got 10! →

Do you know
how many toys
or houses you got
to?

Sincerely Cass[...]

You've Got Questions?
Santa's Got Answers!

Most of my most difficult Santa questions come not in winter but at the close of summer every year. That's when Annie and I take part in one of our favorite Stone Mountain celebrations, the weekend after Labor Day Yellow Daisy Festival, which is billed as the South's largest arts and crafts show. More than four hundred artists and crafty people set up their booths along a series of wide pathways that wind through a wooded section of the park. Annie and I walk around in summer outfits and visit with kids and grown-ups as we go.

The fun part of this adventure is that both of us are kept busy responding to all kinds of questions . . .

"What are you doing here?" Well, I have to be somewhere, and this is one of my favorite places in the whole world.

"Where did you come from?" The stork brought me. OK, not true, but it is a fun answer.

"Where are your reindeer?" That's a favorite question, heard all the time, everywhere. I usually say the deer are at the North Pole—it's much too hot for reindeer in Atlanta in summer. Well, isn't that true?

Then the jackpot: "Are you Santa Claus?" This one always puts me on the spot. Do I say yes or no?

How would a politician answer? "Do I look like Santa Claus? I do? Well, are you being a good kid? Well, if you're being a good kid, that's all that matters, isn't it? If you're being a good kid, it doesn't matter if Santa Claus is watching you, does it? That's why you always have to be good. Right?"

I don't like to stop there though. I'd much rather give them something to believe in, so I tell them what I believe: "Tell me, who's always watching you to make sure you're being good? No, besides Santa. That's right, Jesus is always watching you, not just

the Red Suit Diaries

to make sure you're being good but to watch over you and take good care of you. Right?"

Of course, that leads to more questions from the kids. "How did you get here?" This is an easy one. In a van, which is the straight-up truth again.

But then comes the follow-up: "Why didn't you use the sleigh?" Tough one again, but I love it, because it gives me a chance to share my belief. "Didn't you know that the magic only works on Christmas? That's right, only on Christmas—of course, you can have Christmas in your heart every day. You know why? Do you know what that magic is? It's love—love is what makes Christmas happen. Love is what Christmas is all about—Jesus' birthday, when God proved how much he loved the world, and you and me. He loved us so much that he sent his Son into the world. Then Jesus proved how much he loved us by giving his life for us so that we could have eternal life. That is what Christmas is all about. God and Jesus' love for us, parents' love for their kids, and kids' love for their parents. And on that wonderful, magical night, kids' dreams come true. Reindeer fly and Santa delivers presents to kids all over the world in one night, and it's all because God loves you and me."

Breakfast Is on Me

I am about to describe a scene that is the perfect definition of the word *pandemonium*.

One Macy's tradition has been the Breakfast with Santa event. For years young mothers have been bringing their little ones, dressed up in their Christmas party best, to the downtown Macy's store to have a breakfast with Santa.

When the special events folks at Macy's asked me to be their star at the breakfast, I had a vision of sitting down to eat with a group of kids and having them sit on my lap and tell me what they wanted for Christmas. (What is it about me that always makes me have such an erroneous impression of what life is really going to be like?)

I arrived the first morning and asked the special events person what the format was. She told me the kids were all gathered in the restaurant on the mezzanine. They had been served a French toast and

198   the Red Suit Diaries

syrup breakfast with a glass of milk, and they were being entertained by some furry animals, clowns, and the "Story Lady." I was to go on when the Story Lady had finished. I asked the special events woman what I was to do, and she said to start at the front and work my way to the back by going from table to table, letting the parents take pictures of me with their little ones.

That sounded easy enough. I casually asked how many kids were in there, and she said they had reservations for 217 people, children and adults. *Two hundred and seventeen in that tiny room!*

I had to wait for a little while, and then one of the elves working the room came and said it was time. I walked out of the card shop where I had been hiding and stepped to the door and into the room.

Now it is time for that word again—*pandemonium!* These kids and adults had been crammed into that room for an hour, and all the efforts of the elves, clowns, animals, and the Story Lady had been designed to whip them into a frenzy of anticipation for the arrival of Santa Claus. Then suddenly here he was, in all his red-and-white glory! Here he was, big as life, bigger than life, bigger than anything any of them had expected to see!

The yelling, screaming, and shrieking was deafening. Kids were running toward me and away from me. They were jumping up and down on the floor, the chairs, and even on the tables. Some were hiding under the tables, and some behind their mothers.

I went to the nearest table and stood beside a little girl. Her mother stepped backward to get her camera lined up and stuck her spiked heel into the foot of another mother behind her. More screaming. She finally took the shot, and I moved on to another table, then another table and another table. Flashes were going off all around me.

As I made my way along I noticed that very little of the French toast had been eaten. Milk had been spilled on almost all the tables. I tried to avoid dragging my coat through the mess but wasn't very successful.

There was so much chaos, I finally gave up trying to protect myself from all the little hands grabbing my coat and hugging my leg, and instead just concentrated on getting to all the kids and giving their parents a chance to get a picture.

As I neared the back of the room I noticed that the place seemed to be quieting down. I went around into the corner of the room to get to the last few tables, and finally I was done. I asked the elf if that was all, and she said yes. When we walked back into the main part of the room, I couldn't believe it. All but the last few folks were gone. An eerie quiet was settling over the place.

I checked my Mickey Mouse watch. Fifty-five minutes had passed. It had seemed like a lifetime, but then, it had seemed like just a few minutes too. I had made my way through more than one hundred kids in just fifty-five minutes. Could that be a world record?

I made my way back to the car, and as I was dressing down for the ride home I discovered what had happened to half the milk and syrup that had been served. It was all over my outfit. I was covered with a sheen of syrup from my collar to my boots. The fur around the bottom of my coat was sopped from dragging through the milk on the tables.

There are three to five breakfasts a year, and I've walked into that scene often enough so that I've come to love it. It's very nice to be adored, even if your fans are all less than waist high.

One time we tried the routine a bit differently. I went immediately to the throne chair and took the kids on my lap for the pictures, which took a lot more time. The problem was that I was scheduled to be at another appearance twenty-two miles away immediately following the breakfast. With Macy's normal start time of 9:40, I had scheduled myself to be in the next town at 11:15.

Everything went wrong. We were late getting started. Then at the last minute they changed the format on me. Then the traffic getting out of Macy's parking building got backed up.

I was beginning to panic. I do all I can to be on time for my appointments. I don't want anyone to think I've forgotten about them! I looked at my watch as I paid for parking, and it was already 11:00. I would really have to hustle, but even then, I would still be late. I didn't have a cell phone in the van, so I couldn't let them know that I was on the way.

The traffic was light, and I began to wind up the speed a bit. Then I noticed I was blowing by all the

the $\mathcal{R}$ed Suit Diaries

other cars and looked at the speedometer. I was going over eighty! I never drive that fast, so I slowed down a tad.

As I cleared 285 heading north on I-75, the traffic began thinning out and I began to move it up again. I knew that the fuzz often set up a speed trap at a particular place, so I moved over a couple of lanes so I would blend in. And then there he was, a Georgia state patrolman in a Mustang patrol car! I looked down at the speedometer—eighty again. He had me.

His light came on as I went by, but I didn't slow down. I waited until he was right behind me, then, slowing down slightly, I made my way across the six lanes and pulled off into the emergency lane. I was less than a half mile from my exit!

I put both my hands on the top of the steering wheel, where my red sleeve and white fur cuff would be in plain view, and watched in my mirror as he slowly stepped out of his patrol car, carefully put on his Smokey Bear hat, and ambled leisurely toward my car.

"Come on, Barney, hurry it up!" I muttered to myself.

As he came by the bumper, he stopped for a moment, moved away from the car, and looked into the open window. He stopped again, laughed out loud, and said in the ultimate Southern drawl, "Well! I done it all now. I done stopped Sandy Claws!"

Then he stepped up even with the window and looked in. Seeing my natural beard and overall appearance, he slowly took off his dark glasses, put his arm on my windowsill, and said, "Well, by doggies, it is Sandy Claws!" His breath nearly turned my beard yellow.

I decided that I had nothing to lose by playing out the role, so I said, "OK, here's the way it is. I have two hundred kids right up there in that hotel waiting for me, and I'm already late because I saw two hundred other kids downtown, and it took longer than I had planned. I need to get up there, so write up the ticket as fast as you can so I won't keep them waiting." Then I handed him my license.

"Well, Sandy, let me see what I kin do."

204

I watched in the mirror as he actually hustled back to his car. I figured I was in for around one hundred dollars in fines for this little escapade.

I was looking down into my lap when suddenly he was back at my window. "Well, Sandy," he said, sounding like he had escaped from an old *Dukes of Hazzard* episode, "I cain't stand to keep them young'uns waitin' for ya. So I'm gonna give you a warnin'. Just sign ri-cheer an' you can git on down the road."

I snatched the clipboard out of his hand, signed my name, grabbed my license off the clip, and said, "Now you know how I deliver all those toys in just one night!" I floored it and looked back in the mirror to see him standing there laughing so hard he was slapping his knee.

I'm sure that before he got back in his car, I was out of mine at the hotel and on my way in to make a crowd of kids happy. But I'll guarantee you, none of them was as happy as I was! The red suit really does have magical powers.

Elevators

There must be something about the closeness in an elevator that brings out the strangeness in people. I've found that some of the funniest things that happen to Santa happen in elevators.

It doesn't seem to matter what I'm wearing. It can be a suit, blue jeans and a golf shirt, or whatever. Since I can't take my beard off, it's always out front, just waiting for someone to make some comment.

Once I was visiting Annie when she was in the hospital and got on the elevator at the first floor. As I stepped on, I almost stepped right off again. There were four very rough-looking young men already there, and they looked me up and down appraisingly.

I stood right in front of them, looked each in the eyes, then slowly turned my back to face the door. Then I heard a very soft "Ho, ho, ho" coming from over my left shoulder. I turned and smiled at the biggest one of them and said, "Careful, you're stealing my lines."

He started to snicker and looked down at his feet.

I continued to turn and asked them, "Have you been good little boys?"

To my great shock, they all nodded affirmatively. I reached into my jacket pocket, pulled out four suckers, and passed them around, saying, "Great, keep it up."

Just then the door opened for my floor, and as I stepped off the elevator I turned and waved my finger at them. "Now, don't tell anyone you saw me here, OK?"

When the door closed again and the car started upward, I heard near-hysterical laughter coming from my four new friends.

Not too long after that I was calling on a foundation in downtown Atlanta and had gotten all dressed up in a gray suit. I boarded an already-crowded elevator with some other folks and turned to face the door. It was deathly silent, even though there were at least twelve people in there with me.

All of them were dressed like attorneys or accountants. Then I heard some whispering behind me. Without looking around I said in a strong voice, "It is really him!" There was a slight gasp, then a tentative snicker.

Still not looking around, I said, "And, yes, I do have eyes in the back of my head."

The snickers turned to laughs, and as I stepped off at my floor, I turned and waved, saying, "Merry Christmas to all and to all a good day!"

Travels with Santa

Some say that on a trip the most fun is getting there. But the most fun things happen to Annie and me when we're on the road.

On the way home from one trip, a Honda Civic with Pennsylvania plates flashed by us in a big hurry. Right after it got past us, the brake lights came on and it started to slow down.

I hit the brakes and started to slow down too, but still the Honda was slowing down. When it was next to us, I looked over and saw the passenger rolling down the window. So I rolled mine down too. Then I saw that there were two beautiful coeds in the car, and I wondered what on earth they wanted.

the Red Suit Diaries

Then the passenger raised a camera to her eye and aimed it at us. I smiled real big and gave them a hearty wave. The flash went off, the photographer waved back, and away they went. In moments they were out of sight. And Annie and I had added another happy memory to our list.

That summer while driving in Decatur, we noticed three boys ricocheting around the back of a Volvo station wagon right in front of us. They were punching, gouging, yelling, rolling all over the place, and the driver was barely visible as she hunched over the steering wheel.

Annie decided we needed to give the beleaguered mom a hand and told me to pull alongside the Volvo at the next light. I got right beside them and stopped so I was even with the back of the wagon. Annie got the attention of one of the boys and pointed to me. I leaned forward so he could get a good look, and his smart-aleck smirk disappeared.

He yelled something and scrambled to get into a seat. I made a "shhh" motion with my finger to my lips, and all three of them saw it. In a moment they were all seated in the backseat.

I made a seat-belt buckling motion with both hands, and they began digging for their seat belts. I made another "shhh" motion and pulled forward enough to be even with Mom. She made a praying motion with her hands and mouthed, "Thank you, thank you, thank you."

Not a word had been spoken, but the power of Santa had ruled again.

Home Visits

She wanted a lifetime memory and had planned to record a real visit from Santa with a camera and a camcorder. All she needed was a Santa. And not just any Santa—me! She had scouted around and seen me at Stone Mountain Park, and she had tracked me down through the park public relations folks.

Her kids were a boy of seven and a girl of four. She was sure this was the last year her son would be a believer, and she wanted to preserve the wonder of it for all the Christmases in the future.

Christmas Eve was an important time for my own family. Annie and I would be making an appearance at Mount Carmel during the Christmas Eve service, then we would be going home and having our Christmas that night so we could go to her grandmother's house the next day for a long-standing traditional family Christmas.

But I'm a sucker for kids, so I agreed to go to her house if it could be for a short time early in the evening. She was absolutely gleeful as we discussed and planned the encounter.

On Christmas Eve, I parked the van so I could make a fast getaway, and just before I got out I checked the time. It was exactly 6:00, right on time. I went quietly up the front steps and found a pillowcase with some toys in it right where Mom had said it would be. I went to the front door and eased it open. Dad was standing at the far end of the hall with a camcorder, but he wasn't ready so I backed out, closed the door, then pushed it open again and avoided looking at the camera. But I could see that the tally light was on, so he was recording.

The layout was again just as she described. The hall ran straight to the back and into the kitchen. On my right was a formal dining room, not to be involved in the night's festivities. On my left, through an arched doorway about ten feet down the hall, was the living room where Mom and the kids were waiting, seated together on the couch reading the Christmas story from Luke.

I tiptoed dramatically (for the camera) down the hall and stopped just short of the arched doorway. I eased my face around the corner and peered in. I waited there until the boy looked up and saw me, and then I snatched my face back around the corner.

"Mom, Mom," I heard him say. "I just saw Santa Claus."

"Where?" Mom asked.

Brother responded, "Right there, in the door."

"No, Bobby, you're imagining things. Santa won't be coming until after you're asleep," Mom explained, also reminding me of his name.

I waited a moment and looked around the door again, and this time he was looking right at me.

"There he is!" he screamed, pointing.

I snapped my fingers and stepped into the room. "Well, you caught me, Bobby," I said, walking toward them. "I came by to see if you were asleep so I could

212

leave your gifts. But since you're awake, I'll have to come back later. Oh, what are you reading?"

Mom stood up and said, "We're reading the Christmas story from the Bible, Santa."

"Great," I said, reaching for her Bible. "Can I read some of that? It's my all-time favorite story." She handed me the Bible right on cue and went across the room to get her camera. I sat down on the couch between the kids and started to read to them while Mom was shooting away.

I finished the rest of the story and then looked at my watch. "Oh my goodness, I've got to be going. Now you see why you have to be asleep before the toys get delivered. I would rather visit than work, so you have to be asleep." Then, reaching for the pillowcase, I said, "Oh yes, I did bring you a sample of your gifts." Reaching in, I pulled out an unwrapped toy and handed it to Bobby, and pulled out another toy and handed it to his sister.

I stood and leaned over them and said, "Now, promise me you're going to be good kids. Bobby, are you going to be a good boy?"

He nodded.

"And you're going to be a good girl, right?"

Too late, she was already deep into the new toy. So I headed for the door. I had seen Dad shooting video through the other door into that room and assumed he had stepped back into the hall. When I got to the door to the outside I turned to the camera and said, "Merry Christmas to all and to all a good night!" I laid my finger beside my nose, stepped outside, and closed the door.

I called Mom the day after Christmas and asked if she got what she wanted. She said, "My kids are going to believe in Santa until they are old as the hills, and they have the video to prove he's real. That tape is now our most treasured heirloom. We've already had it duplicated and put the original in our safety deposit box. Thank you, thank you, thank you!"

A couple of years later, I was again asked to spend my Christmas Eve in someone else's house.

This time the caller was a well-known sportscaster whom I'll call Sam. (Of course, that's not his real name.) He had an eight-year-old daughter, Stacy, who was absolutely convinced that her friends were

the Red Suit Diaries

right, that Santa wasn't real. My job was to give her one last great Santa memory.

Sam didn't leave anything to chance. He came to my office and drew a diagram of his house, and we rehearsed an elaborate entry plan. He also drew me a map of how to find his house. (Yes, there were some Xs and Os on both the drawings. After all, he was a sportscaster.) He also told me his wife was not in on his plan and that he would tape it for an instant replay.

I found the house no problem. (It was an X on his big map.) In the carport I found the garbage bag full of toys (an O) and stuffed them into my own red bag. Then I took a (pass) route out the back of the carport, across a big deck, and through a sliding glass door into a sunroom. On the other side of the sunroom I could see the family in the family room.

Beside a roaring fire there was Sam, his wife, and Stacy sitting on the couch that was facing slightly toward the sliding glass door I had to go through into the room. I couldn't believe they hadn't seen me already. I paused to think.

Then Mom announced that she had to stir something that must've been cooking, and she got up off the couch, heading away from me. A moment later Stacy jumped up and followed her. Then Sam got up to stoke the fireplace. He had his back to me. I quickly opened the sliding door, stepped through, and stood frozen, waiting.

A moment later Stacy stepped back into the room from the kitchen. She took two steps, spotted me, and screamed, "Santa!" Sam jumped and nearly fell into the fire as he whirled around. Mom dashed into the room with a dishrag in her hands, and her mouth dropped open into the same shape as Stacy's.

I had my bag in one hand and a big gift in the other. I dropped them both and moved toward Stacy.

"Well, hello, Stacy, how are you doing?" I almost had to pry her feet from the floor. I hugged her and started for the couch. "Wow, it's hot in here. Would you mind if I take off my coat?" I asked politely.

All three of them answered positively at the same time. So I unbuckled my belt, unzipped my coat, and took it off. I had on a ruffled sleeved shirt and a lacy jabot with a red velvet vest to match my coat.

the ℝed Suit Diaries

I lay my coat, belt, and hat carefully across the arm of the chair.

Stacy and I had a near-adult conversation about several things, including a bunch of facts about her cousins, their pets, where they lived, and things I had memorized from Sam's information sheet. She asked me how reindeer fly, and I told her that Christmas night is the most magical night of the year because it commemorates when Jesus was born. She nodded knowingly. I told her Jesus came into the world because God loved us so much that he sent his Son to save us from our sins.

I told her that the most powerful force in the world is love—love between God and Jesus and us, and love between parents and their children. She watched me intently as I spoke, and nodded. She told me what she wanted for Christmas, and I watched as Sam nodded for some things and shook his head once or twice.

I got the message. So I said, "Well, Stacy, you know that not everyone gets everything they want for Christmas. But let's see what we have in the bag for you."

I got up to retrieve the gifts, and there was Mom checking out my coat. "Lined and everything," she said, easing it down. "Nice, very nice."

I smiled at her and said, "Thank you, my elves do a good job."

"It sure looks like they do," she said, shaking her head.

I retrieved the bag and the gift and handed them to Stacy. "I want you to save these until I'm gone; I must get on with the deliveries. You're getting to be a big girl, and I wanted to stop in and let you know that I'm going to depend on your parents for your Christmas gifts from now on. I can see that there is enough love here for them to take very good care of you. I have so many smaller kids, so I'm passing you on to your mom and dad."

Then I said I must be going, and picked up my coat. Stacy's attention had shifted to her gifts, but her mom had a few under-her-breath questions. "Who are you and where are you from? Who sent you?"

Looking furtively around the room but not at the camera that Sam had pointed at us, I leaned forward

the ℞ed Suit Diaries

and whispered, "Santa Claus, and I'm from the North Pole."

"How did you get here? Who sent you?" she insisted, raising her voice a notch.

I leaned forward again as I buckled my belt and said even more quietly, "Weren't you listening? This is the night; this is the most magical night of the whole year! Just relax and go with the magic. Go with the love!"

I turned, slid open the door, stepped through, and was at the van in a flash. According to the clock, I still had time to get home, get Annie, and get to church for the service. Then to humble me and to prove I really am not Santa Claus, I got lost trying to get out of the subdivision. I drove by Sam's house two more times before I stumbled on the route to the main road.

I made it home to get Annie, and we then made it to church in time to do our regular Santa visit at the close of the service. But when we got home after that, I was done in; we decided to have our Christmas later.

Annie was really disappointed that I had messed up our own Christmas to make someone else's happy. It cost me a whole day of shopping at the after-Christmas sale at Macy's! Then she was happy again.

A week or so after Christmas, Sam called to tell me that he finally did tell his wife about our deal. Just before, they had gone to a party where his video had been shown. Everyone became believers!

As much joy as I have hearing people profess belief in the red suit and all it embodies, I hope more for belief in the source of all these things. I hope for mercy and the humility to accept it. I hope for Christmas to come into every heart, and for the faith to keep Christmas every day. I hope for God's gift to be opened and passed along because, as a giver of gifts—and a recipient too—I've seen this truth: There are wonders in his love.

Acknowledgments

A project of this magnitude doesn't happen in a vacuum. Many, many people contributed with their encouragement and their urging me to write down my adventures with their kids.

I must thank my coauthor in life, my wonderful wife, Annie, who is not only the most beautiful Mrs. Claus ever, but is also the most loving human being I know. It was through her love that I came to fully know and understand God's love and learn that I could demonstrate his love to others.

I want to thank Kathy Whitaker, Nancy Dodd, and all the rest of the office staff at Mount Carmel Christian Church who read my first draft and encouraged me to continue and see this effort to conclusion.

Cathy Manack, a Mount Carmel member, school teacher, and now a renowned grammarian, did the first edit and took my words and grammar apart and put them back together again in acceptable English. Thanks, Cathy.

It is my hope that you've found these words entertaining, provoking, and heartwarming. May God have blessed you with the reading of these words. I thank him most of all—the source of all love in these pages.

Officially Santa at Stone Mountain Park for 13 years, **Ed Butchart** founded and operates Friends of Disabled Adults and Children, (FODAC). From a 64,000-square-foot workshop, he directs a full-time staff of 12 and hundreds of volunteers in repairing wheelchairs and other medical equipment for the needy. They've refurbished and provided life-changing equipment for more than 45,000 people with disabilities in 51 countries and 35 states.

Public service and personal work have brought Butchart numerous humanitarian awards, including the Governor of Georgia and Mayor of Atlanta Commendations in 1993, the Dekalb College MLK Jr. Humanitarian Award in 1988, and the Metro Atlanta Council for Exceptional Children "Outstanding Individual" Award in 1998.

Butchart serves as an elder in his church, Mount Carmel Christian, and lives near Atlanta, Georgia, with Mrs. Claus, a.k.a. Annie. They have five adult children.